HOW TO MAXIMIZE YOUR DOG'S POTENTIAL

HOW TO MAXIMIZE YOUR DOG'S POTENTIAL

Training your dogs through love, understanding, and structure.

JORDAN ROGERS

Jordan Rogers
How to Maximize Your Dog's Potential

Published by Spines
1500 Getaway Blvd, Boynton Beach, FL
ISBN: 979-8-89383-191-7

This book was written and dedicated to the memory of the most incredible dog I have ever known, Koda.

Koda passed away on July 15th, 2023, at the age of 11 after suffering a short but intense battle with osteosarcoma, but not before he left me with a lifetime of knowledge and lessons. Through watching Koda and the way he mentored all the new puppies that came into my house, I learned more about dog behavior and interactions than I have from any schooling. He taught them about good behavior in the home and would step in if they were jumping on people or other dogs or got the zoomies in the house, he moderated their play and would help teach them how to properly interact with adult dogs while issuing minimal corrections (to either the puppy or adult dog), and above all, he taught me that patience, understanding, and communicating with the dog in a way that they understand is key to any successful training endeavor. Overall, Koda proved to me that structure, guidance, and only using corrections when absolutely necessary, was all you needed to train a dog.

On top of all his tireless efforts to help new puppies, he was also a therapy dog for anyone who was lucky enough to know him. Koda felt and saw everything, and whether you were so angry you were throwing things, or so sad you couldn't pull yourself off the floor, you could guarantee that he was going to be there to pull you out of it. He not only helped people feel loved and important, but he also helped many people and dogs overcome their fear of dogs, just by being a giant, scary looking dog, with the heart and presence of an angel.

For me personally, he taught me what true love really is. When I was anxious, he was my weighted blanket; when I was happy, he was my adventure buddy; when I was sad, he was my source of a smile and a shoulder to lean on; when I was angry, he grounded me; when I was scared, he was my protector; and even when I made mistakes, he was my number one supporter. No matter where I went or what I did, he was always right there beside me. Koda wasn't a fighter, but he was for me and his brothers, and he saved each of us at one time or another. You were never safer or felt more loved than when Koda was around. He also showed a girl who tried to avoid children how precious they really are, and that they should be loved and protected at all costs, while being the gentlest guardian of any child he met.

To say that Koda is missed would be an understatement, and his contributions to the people and dogs he impacted will forever be remembered.

I love you, Koda.

Thank you for saving me and for everything you taught me along the way.

ADVANCE PRAISE

"I cannot recommend Jordan, our dog trainer, highly enough! Her incredible skills and dedication have transformed our once-unmanageable German Shorthaired Pointer/Lab mix, Lola, into a fantastic and well-behaved family dog. Jordan's innovative methods saved Lola's life and have made a lasting impact on our entire household.

From the start, Jordan exhibited unparalleled expertise. Lola's challenging behaviors, including defiance and aggression, were met with Jordan's deep understanding of canine cognition. She crafted a personalized training program that not only addressed Lola's unique needs but also enlightened us about the importance of mental stimulation alongside physical exercise.

What sets Jordan apart is her unwavering commitment. She tackled one of the most challenging cases she had encountered, working tirelessly to achieve remarkable results. Her patience and dedication were truly commendable.

Jordan's communication skills were also outstanding. She was always available to answer our questions, provide guidance, and offer support whenever we needed it. Her responsiveness and willingness to share her expertise made the entire training process a positive and empowering experience for us as pet owners.

Beyond her professional skills, Jordan developed a wonderful relationship with Lola, and the positive impact endures to this day. Lola, once a defiant and aggressive puppy, is now a lovable and well-behaved family dog who seamlessly coexists with our three other labs.

Jordan's influence on Lola's life is immeasurable, and her recent book is a testament to her expertise. I wholeheartedly recommend Jordan to anyone seeking a dog trainer of the highest caliber. Her insights and methods are not only effective but also inspiring.

It is with high regard that I can attest to Jordan's exceptional skills, commitment, and the success stories she creates are deserving of widespread recognition. Thank you, Jordan, for making a profound difference in our lives and Lola's. You truly are an exceptional dog trainer!

Catherine Brigger - happy dog owner of 4"

DISCLAIMER

This book, as well as all training advice from our trainers and videos, are being provided to you for educational purposes only. We are not responsible for anything you do, or do not do, with your dog or any other dog, and we are not responsible for the outcomes of those actions, or lack thereof. Rather, we are only giving you the tools to understand and be able to work with dogs.

We have no intention, need, or desire to try and sway you towards or away from any training methods or tools out there. Rather, we aim to teach you how to properly utilize every training tool and technique. When in doubt, it is always better to know how to use something properly and never use it, than it is to not know and do it incorrectly or allow a dog to be injured.

Please know, if you are completely against everything except positive reinforcement, then this book probably is not for you. We will not be fielding any negative comments or complaints from people with varying viewpoints, as this book is being provided for educational purposes only, and we want to ensure that people are getting complete information.

FOREWORD

I met Jordan Rogers while studying for my dog training certification. I quickly realized how incredibly fortunate I was to be paired with Jordan as my training mentor. She became an essential part of my education and understanding of dog behavior. Jordan shared her knowledge with me and encouraged me to learn even more than what the program had to offer. Watching her successfully work with dogs on various goals was truly inspiring. She has an understanding and a way of connecting with dogs unlike anything I've ever seen before. Always supportive, Jordan was a reliable and consistent mentor. She provided me with a valuable learning experience that far exceeded any expectations I could have had. Jordan also has the biggest heart and the most genuine love for dogs. When our puppy Luna became increasingly reactive, Jordan did not hesitate for a second to offer her help. She took Luna into her home to help her through her fears. She also supported my family in learning how to manage and respond to a fear-reactive puppy. Our girl Luna has made significant progress and leads a much happier life now. Jordan helped us see beyond challenging behaviors and understand where they came from and how to respond appropriately and effectively. We are forever grateful for her knowledge, compassion, and support.

Jordan's understanding of dog behavior and her ability to modify behaviors is incredible. I'm so excited that she is now sharing her mentoring experience and training expertise through Koda's Canine Academy! I've learned so much from her already and consider myself fortunate to have the opportunity to work alongside Jordan.

Billie Lawrence

CONTENTS

SECTION THREE:
TEACHING THE OBEDIENCE CUES

SECTION ONE:
EVERYTHING YOU SHOULD KNOW ABOUT DOGS

BRINGING HOME A NEW PUPPY

Have you been thinking about bringing home a new puppy? Or do you have a client who is thinking about getting a new puppy and needs tips on bringing it home? If so, there are some easy things you can do to help your puppy settle in quicker and avoid potential problems in the future.

1. If possible, take something that smells like their litter mates/mother home with them:
When you first bring a puppy home, they can sometimes have anxiety because it is the first time they have ever been away from their mother or siblings. Having something that smells like their mother/siblings to put in their kennel can help them relax and settle into the new setting faster.

Another thing I like to do is warm up water and then put it in an empty two-liter bottle, then wrap it in whatever I took from their mother/siblings. Not only will it smell like them but be warm and comforting.

2. Go straight home when you pick them up and avoid "showing them off":
Taking them away from the only home they have ever known is

already a huge shock, so try not to add insult to injury by taking a bunch of pit stops along the way.

Take your pup home, let them adjust to being in their new environment and safe space, and then start taking them out to meet new people and see new things.

Socialization is great and I highly recommend it but allowing them to have a few days to settle into their new environment is important too, so that they feel comfortable around you and confident that you will keep them safe.

Socialization and exposure will be much easier when the puppy has realized that you are their new safe space, and that they will be safe if you are there with them.

3. Set the puppies stuff up before you bring them home:

Your house is a huge place, so make the puppies area before you ever come home, that way it is comfortable and gives them a safe space. You can do this by using a small puppy play pen and filling it with their bed/crate, toys, and food/water bowls so that they have a space all their own. Not only does this give you a safe space to leave them when you are not able to keep eyes on them but allows them to get familiar with their new space in a safe way before you put them in the kennel to sleep for the first night.

4. Introduce them to other dogs outside the home:

If you already have a dog at home, try introducing them to the new puppy outside of the house, where they are less likely to be territorial. Then, they will not feel like you are just "bringing a strange dog" into their space but introducing a new friend. Once the dogs have gotten familiar with one another, take them into the house together.

From here I always try to let dogs interact with as little interference as possible, as dogs will teach one another where they fall within their "pack" and have their own ways of communicating what is and isn't appropriate behavior towards them. Obviously, if you feel like the puppy is in danger then you should step in, but it is normal for adult dogs to act "rude" towards young puppies as they are teaching them what are appropriate interactions between adult dogs.

Often, I see people who do not allow their dogs to interact the way dogs normally would, and this creates animosity and issues within their pack order.

Remember, your older dog has just as much right to set their own boundaries as you do, and we cannot be the ones who set those boundaries for them. Rather, we help mediate and ensure that both pups stay safe throughout the process.

5. Try to set the precedent for your expectations for their behavior right from the beginning:

Whatever it is you want your puppy to do as an adult, start teaching it right from the beginning. The puppy stage only lasts for a short period of time and before you know it, they will be an adult. Suddenly, the cute jumping on you when you get home and nipping during playtime isn't so cute, and you could have a real problem on your hands.

Since we know that those behaviors aren't something we want in our adult dogs, why would we allow it when they are babies? When you bring a puppy home they have a clear mind for molding, so if you teach them exactly what you want right from the beginning then they will never know anything different.

This will help you avoid having to break problem behaviors in the future while simultaneously trying to teach them new things.

6. Playing the name game, the puppy recall game, potty training, and crate training are all things that should start on the first day they come home:

Not only will this help your puppy settle into a new routine faster, but it will give you a way to get their attention and hopefully get them back to you if needed.

Don't be fooled! Even 6-week-old puppies can be taught their name and can respond to movement and excited noises like the puppy recall game, so it is never too soon to start and the longer you wait the harder it will be!

Now that we have covered all the basics, here is a very simple checklist you can use to make sure you have everything you need before you bring your puppy home, as well as some things you should take into consideration to ensure you are prepared when the time comes.

NEW PUPPY CHECKLIST

1. An established home vet office with appointments set to get puppy vaccines and deworming.
2. Food and water bowls
3. Food
4. Collar / Harness
5. Identification Tags / Microchip
6. Leash
7. Long line
8. Bed
9. Crate
10. Chew bones / toys
11. Brushes / other necessary grooming equipment
12. Treats (training and regular)
13. Poop Bags

THINGS TO CONSIDER:

1. How much time will the puppy spend in the crate each day, and what is your plan for being able to let them potty during the day while working on potty training?
2. If you are not able to go home to let them out, what resources are available to do so in your area?
3. How much free time do you have throughout the day, and what is your plan to ensure that your dog is getting enough physical and mental stimulation?

4. If you do not plan on doing the grooming, what local grooming options do you have?
5. Do you plan on training them yourself, and if not, what are your local options?
6. If you must leave the puppy somewhere overnight, who will take care of them?

IMPORTANCE OF EXPOSURE

WHY IS EXPOSURE IMPORTANT?

PROPER EXPOSURE IS ONE OF THE BEST THINGS WE CAN DO FOR our dogs to help set them up for success. The more new things we can expose them to while they are still young, in a proper and positive way, the more likely they are to not be fearful in the future and be able to go to more places without issues.

While most trainers focus primarily on socialization, such as being okay around all types of people and other dogs, socialization is only a small piece of the pie when we are looking to make our dogs solid around new distractions and situations.

Exposure involves introducing our dogs to all sorts of sounds, items, experiences, and situations to help them learn how to control their emotional reactions to new things and be calm and confident in any setting they are thrust into. Yes, socialization falls into this category as well, but it does not cover all the ground necessary to produce a truly confident dog.

Once you have finished reading this, please take the time to look at the Exposure Checklist for an example of a list of items that dogs could potentially be exposed to. Obviously, there might be more things that you want your dog to be okay with, but this list should give you a good idea of how to get going.

COMMON MISTAKES IN EXPOSURE

Perhaps the biggest mistake people make when trying to expose their dogs to new things is throwing them in too quickly without preparing the dog properly first. We must remember that dogs can be fearful of things we might not expect them to be, so we never want to push them over their fear threshold, as this could result in a lifetime of fear for that item or situation. Rather, we want to move slowly, at the dog's pace, and ensure that they can calmly accept all the new things we are presenting to them. By moving slowly, we can make more progress quickly, because we will not run the chance of building a negative association with something that would then take counterconditioning to fix.

Another common mistake is getting too excited when introducing dogs to new things, such as using too high-value treats, requiring your dog to look at you all the time and ignoring the item, or getting your dog playfully agitated. By doing these things it will make them more likely to ignore the items you were trying to expose them to in the first place, and not allow us the opportunity to conquer their comfortability around them. Rather, we want them to be able to interact calmly with the things we are exposing them to and learn to stay calm instead of ignoring them all together.

Finally, we never want to use any sort of aversive training method while we are doing exposure work. Aversive methods tend to use fear or pain as a reinforcer, which could cause the dog to try and hide their emotions to avoid corrections, resulting in unsafe outbursts at inappropriate times as they continue to be pushed past their fear threshold. In other words, NEVER REPRIMAND A DOG FOR BEING SCARED. Everyone is afraid of different things, and it's our job to help them learn that they don't need to be scared and that as long as they default back to us, they will remain safe.

USING THE ENGAGE/DISENGAGE GAME

One of the best techniques for doing proper exposure is playing the engage/disengage game. The result of this game is that your dog will be able to look at something potentially scary, new, unusual, or disturbing, and then still redirect back to you for guidance. This is the ideal response in so many different training situations, as we want our dogs to know that regardless of what is going on around them, they will be safe and have guidance from us on how to handle it.

Before you begin trying to expose your dog to new items, you will want to ensure that you have already built an association between either your clicker or mark word and a food treat, as this is what we will use to reward them for the calm behaviors they are presenting to us (Please refer to Section 3 Chapter 1).

To start training the engage/disengage game, you will want to take your dog somewhere that has a low-mild level of distractions, such as the side of a somewhat busy street or even a local park. Then, every time something distracting walks by, you will mark and reward them for looking at the distraction. Soon, your dog will learn that looking at a new distraction will get them rewarded. While doing this, we want to remember to keep the training sessions short (5-10 min), as often dogs will get overwhelmed by all the new stimuli quickly. You want to repeat your exposure training several times, over a series of days, until they no longer react in an emotional way to them.

Once the dog knows that they will be rewarded for engaging with something, we want to work on the disengage aspect. Now, instead of marking and rewarding them for simply looking at it, we will wait until they look at the new item, say their name, and wait for them to look back at us (looking for the treat) to mark and reward that behavior. This is teaching the dog that when something unexpected happens, they should notice it and then immediately check in with us for guidance.

If the dog will not redirect from the item to you, start slowly moving backwards, applying gentle pressure to the leash while encouraging them with high pitched noises. This should be enough to get them to disengage and redirect to you, at which point you will mark and reward that behavior. If you notice that the dog seems to be failing to redirect more than they are succeeding, then you have likely passed their behavior threshold. Therefore, you should try to move further away from whatever you are trying to redirect them from until they are able to successfully do so without you having to always apply pressure on the leash.

If you are working on this exercise with a dog who has already become leash reactive, then you might need to utilize the emergency U-turn. Essentially, this means that if your dog starts to bark, lunge, or growl at the end of their leash, you will immediately turn and start walking in the other direction, while using high pitched noises to entice them. Just as before, the second your dog disengages and turns towards you, you will mark and reward that behavior. Then, you will turn around and head back towards the stimulus. As soon as you see them start getting reactive again (ears forward and erect, body stiff, quickened pace, or excess panting), you will once again take them in the other direction and disengage them. The key is, we want to disengage them before they pass their threshold and get reactive so that we can reward them for calm behavior. As you do this exercise, you should notice that you can slowly get closer and closer with each approach without your dog becoming reactive.

THE IMPORTANCE OF BODY LANGUAGE

As you should know by now, our dogs' body language is the most important thing we can pay attention to when we are doing exposure exercises.

Since our dogs are not able to verbally tell us when they are scared, it is our responsibility to pick up on these physical cues, and then adjust our training accordingly to ensure that we are not pushing them past their fear threshold.

In general, here are the most obvious physical signs that our dog is scared or stressed:

1. Licking their lips excessively
2. Yawning a lot
3. Grabbing treats rougher than usual
4. Putting their tail between their legs
5. Cowering
6. Panting excessively and maybe starting to drool
7. Looking away pointedly and refusing to make eye contact.
8. Showing the whites of their eyes
9. Shaking (whether it is a tremble or physical shake)
10. Trying to leave the situation.

If you see any of these behaviors, then you are either too close or moving too quickly. Try moving back 10-20 feet or starting with a less scary distraction or environment. If we push them past their threshold, the dogs will start to shut down.

Unfortunately, for most people, this can be masked by what appears to be a very well-behaved dog. They will generally be sitting or standing there doing nothing, looking at nothing, and just existing, which is a very bad sign. This means that your dog has reached its limit and has shut down their emotions all together because they are too stressed, and they don't know what else to do.

Once your dog has reached this point, they will likely be even more scared or worried about the things they are experiencing because they have learned that even when they are trying to tell you that they are scared, you aren't going to listen. Eventually, you will have to go back and do all sorts of counter-conditioning to fix it, creating more work for you and them in the long run.

TIPS FOR GETTING STARTED:

1. Keep it light, keep it easy, and keep the overall stimulation level low and below threshold.
2. If your dog ever shows signs of stress or fear, back off until they are calm, happy, and easily taking treats.
3. If you are working on a new surface or location, the engage/disengage game isn't very applicable. Instead, work on

easy obedience or tricks that the dog enjoys doing while exposing them to the surface or location.

4. The earlier you start the better! While exposure is good for dogs of all ages, their brains are particularly malleable prior to four months of age, so this is the prime time for proper exposure. You may need to do it again later, especially as fear stages occur, but by starting early we are giving their brains a wider range of "normal" things they might encounter.

WHAT IMPACTS A DOG'S TRAINABILITY?

When we are talking about how something is going to impact a dog's training, just knowing their breed isn't enough, as not all dogs will act or respond the same just because of their breed. Yes, a lot of what motivates them will be similar and you might notice certain behaviors that occur more with certain breeds than others. However, you should never assume anything about a dog. They should all be treated as individuals when approaching their training and we need to adjust our training plans accordingly for each. Therefore, whenever I am working with a dog for the first time, I am looking for specific things:

1. What motivates them?

For some dogs it is food, some toys, and some just praise, but knowing what motivates them is always important. Remember, just because something motivates one dog doesn't mean it will motivate another, and the dog decides what motivates them, not us.

2. What distracts them?

A lot of times, these are common traits amongst breeds, but not always. For example, if you are working with a scent hound outside in the grass, you can expect that they will probably be distracted by any new scent in the area, so, you would want to make sure that the treats aren't just high value, but stinky, or consider working inside first where there are less new smells.

3. What is their activity level?

Yes, a lot of breeds tend to be high energy genetically, such as Labradors, Siberian Huskies, and German Shepherds, but not all of them are. Therefore, the same way that you would approach a training plan with a high energy lab might not be the same way you approach one with a lazy lab, as one will likely need a lot more mental/physical stimulation than the other one to remain content in the home.

4. What is their temperament?

When we are working with certain breeds, owners, and trainers alike, will often get into the mindset that "they are a working breed, so they can handle tougher training.

However, this can be detrimental to a dog and their training, so I always like to refer to dogs as being either soft, neutral, or hard. If a dog is "soft", then they are the ones who are timid, respond only to positive training methods, and will shut down if any sort of aversive is introduced, including a harsh tone.

My dog Hershey, who is a chocolate lab, is a perfect example of this. If you so much as raise your voice when you are working with him, or if he can get even a whiff of frustration, he will shut down and be completely unresponsive to training. If a dog is "hard", then they are typically much more outgoing, independent, and require a firmer hand when they are training, because they are usually the "give them an inch and they take a mile" type.

My dog, Koda, who was half German Shepherd half Husky, would fall into this category. Yes, he responds well to positive reinforcement, but he is also smart enough to know that if you aren't looking, he can do whatever he wants, and he is not interested in working for anything other than food.

Finally, my dog Bruce, who is a mix of a bunch of different bully and working breeds, would fall into the neutral category. He responds very well to all types of training, making him easy to work with for the most part, and when I have had to correct him, he has only ever needed to be told he couldn't do something once.

5. Do they want to work?

If you are working with breeds that were bred to work independently of humans (huskies, great Pyrenees, most terriers), they tend to be a little more independent, resistant to training, and some might even say stubborn.

This isn't for a lack of brains, it's because they were bred to work without much guidance. Therefore, keeping training short, fun, and engaging will work best.

The same would apply for a lot of breeds that weren't bred to work at all, such as most dogs that fall in the toy group.

Meanwhile, there are a lot of breeds that were bred to work by the direction of their handler (labs, German Shepherds, Belgium Malinois) which inherently gives them not just a higher work drive, but a higher drive to please their handler.

However, because these dogs were bred to work, they also tend to require a lot more work, and work that challenges them mentally, so they don't seek fulfillment elsewhere.

6. What triggers them?

Knowing what a dog will and won't react towards is probably one of the most important things to know about them. This is how we will be able to set them up for success, and what we will need to work on the most.

Learning a dog's triggers, and how to help them control their emotional reactions to those triggers, will help not only you as the trainer, but the dog be able to remain calm in more situations.

7. How old are they?

When working with a young dog who has no prior associations with anything, it is usually much easier to teach them new things without much difficulty. However, as dogs get older and older, they build more and more associations, as well as bad behaviors that need help.

Knowing this ahead of time will help you establish their training plan because you will have an idea of what they already know and what they don't, and what the best way to approach those things will be.

8. What's their background?

More times than not, how the dog started their life is going to have a huge impact on the way they respond to training. Were they socialized properly? Were they abused? Abandoned? The list goes on and on, but all these different factors will help you identify what the best approach to their training will be.

For example, if you have a dog who was abandoned or abused, odds are you will have to wait a couple of days for them to settle in and get comfortable before you are able to get much done, since trust goes a long way in training a fearful dog.

INTRODUCTION TO HOW DOG'S LEARN

Before we begin teaching our dogs obedience cues, it is important that we take the time to understand the way dogs learn. While there are a lot of big scientific terms that break down exactly how, on a very basic level, dogs learn by association.

Associative learning means that they associate certain actions and behaviors with the consequences and/or rewards that follow them, and then their future actions and behaviors are based on those associations. For example, if you ask your dog to sit and give them a treat, they will associate sitting with getting a treat and will be more likely to repeat that behavior (sitting) in the future.

However, if you were to ask them to sit and then shock them, they would associate sitting with being shocked and be less likely to repeat that behavior (sitting) in the future. Therefore, everything we do when we are working with our dogs is important because we could be making a lifelong association with that behavior.

Building off this principle of learning by association, dog training can be broken into four smaller principles, which implement different techniques to help us change a dog's behavior through positive and negative association.

While each one of these principles has a time and place, the most important rule of thumb to remember is this:

You should never use more force than what is absolutely necessary to correct a behavior while ensuring the health and safety of the dog at all times.

As I said earlier, it only takes one bad experience to completely ruin a dog's perspective of something, including you. Therefore, the use of any corrections or harsh training methods should always be done with extreme caution and under the direction of an experienced trainer. Now, let's review these basic training principles and how we can apply them to dog training.

****IMPORTANT NOTE****

When we are talking about positive and negative in dog training, I want you to think of positive as in "the addition of" (+) **not** as in "good" or "rewarding", and I want you to think of negative as in "the removal of" (-) **not** as in "bad" or "punishing". Therefore, when you see the word positive you will know that something is being added to the scenario, and when you see the word negative you will know that something is being taken away. Then, when we are talking about punishment vs reinforcement, you just need to remember that punishment is always used with the intent to decrease a behavior, and reinforcement is intended to increase that behavior.**

PRINCIPLE 1: POSITIVE REINFORCEMENT

Adding something that the dog finds rewarding increases the likelihood of that behavior repeating. While teaching obedience cues, this is the main principle we will be operating under, as the more positive associations we can build with working, the better.

EX 1: If we give them a treat (something rewarding) after they sit down it will increase the likelihood that they will sit again, because they know a reward is going to follow. We have now built a positive association with sitting.

EX 2: If we give the dog lots of praise and love (something rewarding) after completing a recall when being called inside it will increase the likelihood of them coming again in the future because they received such high praise. We have now built a positive association with coming.

PRINCIPLE 2: NEGATIVE PUNISHMENT

Removing something that the dog finds rewarding decreases the likelihood of that behavior repeating. Generally, with attention seeking behaviors, negative punishment is the most effective because we are removing what the dog finds most rewarding (our attention).

EX 1: If we remove our attention (something rewarding) from the dog while they are jumping on us, they will be less likely to want to jump on us in the future as we have removed their reward for jumping (our attention). We have now built a negative association with jumping.

EX 2: If we are working on food bowl exercises and they break their sit-stay, we will remove the food bowl (something rewarding) so they can't get it, making them less likely to break that sit-stay in the future so they do not lose their reward (food bowl). We have now built a negative association with breaking their position early.

PRINCIPLE 3: NEGATIVE REINFORCEMENT

Removing something that the dog finds unrewarding increases the likelihood that they will repeat that behavior. Whenever we use negative reinforcement, it is important that we still reward the dog once they have corrected their behavior.

EX 1: The dog has already been taught recall, and knows what is expected of them, so now we are using an e-collar to solidify it off-leash around distractions. The moment the dog chooses not to listen to your come command, you would apply constant stimulation until the dog comes back to your side. As soon as they make it back to you, you would let off the stimulation (removing something unrewarding) and reward them for coming to increase the likelihood that they will not ignore you again in the future. We have now built a negative association with choosing to ignore you and a positive association with recall.

EX 2: The dog is walking on a choke chain, and the harder he pulls, the more pressure is applied to the collar. Then, when he slows down a little and the leash is loose, the pressure from the collar releases (removing something unrewarding) and we can reward him for walking nicely on a loose leash, making him more likely to walk on a loose leash in the future to get the reward (foot treat) and avoid the consequence of pulling (pressure on collar). We have now built a negative association with pulling and a positive association with walking nice.

PRINCIPLE 4: POSITIVE PUNISHMENT

Adding something that the dog finds unrewarding decreases the likelihood of that behavior happening again. This should be used as minimally as possible, and only if determined necessary for the safety of the dog or its owner.

EX 1: When a dog is on an electric fence and they get too close to the boundary line, the collar will beep and then eventually shock them (adding something unrewarding) until they retreat to the safety of the yard. (When teaching them the boundary, you should stay outside with them so when they hear the beep, you can recall them back into the yard and get a reward teaching them that when they hear the beep, they need to retreat.) This makes them less likely to try and cross that boundary and more likely to stay in the yard. We have now built a negative association with crossing their yard boundary and a positive association with staying in the yard.

EX 2: If a dog gets into the habit of jumping over a fence, you must make the action of jumping over the fence unrewarding for them, otherwise they will continue to do it. So, we would put an e-collar on them in the morning so they get used to it being on and forget about it, then leave them outside as you normally would, while you stay inside and watch them. We do not want the dog to see us outside or know that the correction is coming from us, as we want them to believe that the shock is coming from the fence itself to make that action unrewarding. As soon as they jump on the fence, you will apply enough stimulation (adding something unrewarding) that they will retreat from the fence immediately, making them less likely to try and jump the fence in the future. We have now built a negative association with jumping the fence.

When looking at the basic training principles, there is something I want you to notice, and that is how we progress through the principles. They went from being the least to the most aversive and this process is known as the LIMA training method, or Least Intrusive Minimally Aversive. When in doubt, this is how you should pursue your training. If positive reinforcement doesn't work, try negative punishment, then negative reinforcement, and then finally positive punishment. If your dog does not already know what it is they are or aren't supposed to do, or what is going to get them rewarded, you **CANNOT** use negative reinforcement or positive punishment, as they will have no idea what you are punishing them for and will not be able to change their behavior. Rather, your dog is likely going to shut down and become non-responsive, as they cannot figure out what to do to avoid receiving further punishment.

In other words:

Punishing them more will not make them learn faster if they do not know what they are being punished for.

For example, if you have never taught your dog recall before, and they do not know that you expect them to come back to you when you say it, adding a correction will not make them suddenly know what recall means.

So, first we need to teach them what it is we want and make sure they know what that is, and then we are disciplining their choice to not listen, and not their lack of knowledge or understanding of what we want.

Now that we have gone over all the basic training principles and understand the techniques we are going to use to teach our dogs various things, let's go over some tips I believe are important to making sure all your training endeavors are successful.

1. Never end a training session on a failed attempt and always end the session on something where the dog was successful, even if you must take a step backwards.

This is known as "going back to Kindergarten" in the dog training world. Simply put, if you need to make something easier for them for a couple attempts to help them be successful, do it! Whether that means you are decreasing the distractions, expecting a shorter duration, or you just switch to something easier all together so you have a chance to reward them, our dog's success should be our main priority.

2. Always work to increase the duration of an exercise before trying to add too many distractions or distance between you and your dog.

These are known as the three Ds of dog training: duration, distance, and distractions.

Duration refers to the amount of time your dog can hold one cue and will be the first "D" we work on in our training, as patience and focus on you is the most important first step for most dogs. Distance refers to how far away you can get from your dog and still have them be responsive to cues. Distractions refer to working them around all different people, places, things, and situations.

All of these should be progressed slowly, ensuring that the dog always stays successful, so you should never try to manipulate more than one of these aspects at a time so that if they fail, it is easier for you to determine why and what you need to do to set them up for success on their next attempt.

3. Do not give your cue unless you know that they are going to respond.

The reason we use the lure to teach a dog the behavior before we introduce the cue is because we do not want our cue to become "poisoned". Poisoning the cue means that we use it before the dog knows what it means, so they end up ignoring it out of ignorance. This can make it very difficult to train them to respond to that cue since they have already learned that they can ignore it or that they do not have to respond the first time you give it. Therefore, if you think you might have poisoned one or more of your cues, it would be a good idea to pick new ones and start the training process over.

4. Keep lessons short and successful, and remember, any progress is good progress.

One of the most common issues I see at mainstream board and train kennels is their approach to lessons with the dog. Rather than treating each dog as an individual and progressing them at a speed appropriate to them, they will put them on the same blanket training plan and push and push to make certain goals each day. Unfortunately, this often leads to a regression in training as the dog starts to shut down because he is not progressing "fast enough" and therefore stops receiving rewards.

With all the dogs I have ever trained, one thing I know to be true is this: if you break down training sessions into smaller and super rewarding sessions and stop when you see them starting to get tired, the dog will always be well rested, eager to work with you, and will retain more information from session to session.

5. Never assume that your dog knows something. If you haven't taken the time to teach them yet, how are they supposed to know?

This is perhaps the most important rule to remember, yet it is sometimes the hardest, even for me. I think it comes from the level of comfortability we get with our dogs and their behavior, and we just expect them to know certain things because "why wouldn't they", forgetting that dogs have the cognitive learning abilities of a toddler. Therefore, if you have never taken the time to teach them something specifically, even something small like getting into the trash in the bathroom for the first time, then you cannot be mad at them.

I know you might be thinking, well, they know that they aren't supposed to get in the kitchen trash so they should know not to get into the bathroom trash either. BUT this is our human mentality building associations on the behalf of our dog, because odds are, the association with the kitchen trash to the bathroom trash was never made in the dog's head, and we never taught it to them. So, rather than getting mad about what they did, we should use it as a learning opportunity and a chance to set our expectations for their behavior in the future.

TIPS TO BEING A GOOD DOG HANDLER

Working with dogs can be challenging, especially for new owners and trainers who do not have as much experience working with a variety of dogs and issues. It can be frustrating and overwhelming trying to work through difficult situations, and sometimes slow or a lack of progress can make you feel as though you aren't doing a good job. However, there are a couple things you should always keep in mind when you are working with dogs so that you can set yourself up for success and be more capable of addressing the issues at hand.

Tip 1: Answer each of the questions on the "what impacts a dog's trainability" list and then create a training plan based on those items.

If we can determine all those items up front, we will have a much better idea of how to best communicate with them during training.

Tip 2: You need to stay calm and under control in every situation.

Our dog is constantly feeding off the energy we are giving off, so whether you are calm and confident or stressed and manic, our dogs will follow suit. Therefore, never work with a dog if you are already frustrated or upset. Instead, take some time to rest and reset, and then come back and try to work with them once you have your own emotions under control.

Tip 3: Any progress is good progress, especially at the beginning.

Yes, a plan is good and will help ensure that your training continues to progress, but deviating from the plan is okay too if it means making the dog successful!

Tip 4: Never be afraid to ask for help or admit that you don't have the skills necessary to help a certain dog.

Not only will this make you appear as a more credible owner and trainer but it will keep you from taking on clients and dogs outside your skill set and give you the opportunity to learn new things. Especially as a dog trainer, the worst thing you can do is promise someone that you can help, take their money, and then not actually be able to help them. Not only will this likely ruin your reputation with that client, but also potentially with other trainers and clients in your area.

GROUP CLASS OR PRIVATE TRAINING?

I get a lot of people that ask me if I think taking their puppy to a training class is a good idea. My answer? Absolutely. Training classes are a great way for you and your pup to learn how to work together as a team, learn new skills, and socialize your dog with other dogs who are probably close to the same age. However, not all training classes are the same and they do not always address specific issues you might be having with your dog.

Therefore, my best recommendation to you is to research ALL the training facilities and INDIVIDUAL trainers near your location and see who/where is going to be the best fit for your dog, yourself, and your lifestyle!

FOR EXAMPLE:

If you have already had success teaching your dog basic skills like sit, down, shake, and stay, but you are really struggling with things like potty and crate training, off-leash recall, or behavior issues, then you should probably consider individual training or a board and train scenario.

Group classes focus a lot more on fundamental skills, and less on individual issues and behaviors.

When in doubt, there are a lot of trainers (like me) that are willing to do short evaluations with you and your dog to see where a good place for you to start might be, so take advantage of it!

When it comes to training dogs you can never assume the "one size fits all" mentality, because that is hardly ever the case, and you deserve to get the most out of every training experience!

If you still aren't sure, there are a couple of easy questions to ask yourself that can help you determine what type of training will be best for you and your pup!

Question	If yes.	If No..
Do you want to focus primarily on behavioral issues?	Private lessons	Group Lessons
Is your dog socialized and used to working around other dogs?	Group or Private	Group Lessons (great opportunity to work on it)
Is your dog reactive?	Private Lessons	Group Lessons (reactivity should be addressed first)
Does your dog work well around distractions?	Group or Private	Group Lessons (good chance to work around distractions)
Do you want to work on more advanced training techniques?	Private lessons or an advanced obedience class/CGC Prep	Group Lessons
Do you want one on one time with the trainer?	Private lessons	Group Lessons
Is your dog less than a year old?	Group Lessons (great chance to socialize and learn to work around distractions)	Private or Group
Is your schedule flexible?	Private or Group	Private (group lessons can be hard to dedicate to if you are working crazy hours)
Are you looking for the most bang for your buck?	Group Lessons (usually, you get more classes for a lower price)	Private (tend to be more expensive, but get more one on one time)
Do you want multiple people to be involved in the training?	Private Lessons (group lessons are usually pretty full and hectic as it is, and they will have limits on how many people can attend)	Group Lessons

SECTION TWO:
CREATING GOOD HOUSE MANNERS

CRATE TRAINING – WHY YOU SHOULD

A LOT OF DOG OWNERS ARE HESITANT TO PUT THEIR DOGS IN kennels because they think it is torturous to keep them in such a confined space. But the truth is, there are many benefits to crate training your dog, and if you start working on it as soon as they come home, they will learn to see the crate not as a punishment, but as a safe space only for them. It will provide you with peace of mind that they are safe while you are not home, and it will teach them how to be okay being alone without finding a bunch of "distractions" to keep them occupied. Now let's discuss not only the reasons why you should crate train your dog, but some things to avoid building a negative association with it!

REASONS YOU SHOULD CRATE TRAIN YOUR DOG:

1. Dogs like to have a safe space that is all theirs they can retreat to, such as a den.

That is why dogs are so naturally drawn to dog houses, closets, and hiding in other small, confined spaces. Therefore, by providing them with a crate that is all theirs, you have given them the safe space they need while ensuring that they are not able to get into anything that could potentially harm them throughout the day.

2. It gives you peace of mind that your dog is not only safe, but that your house is not being destroyed while you are away for any given amount of time.

Remember, puppies are like toddlers and there are all sorts of things they can get into that could be potentially hazardous to them. So, if you wouldn't trust a toddler running around unsupervised all day, you shouldn't trust your puppy!

3. It is not permanent!

Just because you teach your dog how to be in a crate does not mean it is a life sentence for them. All four of my dogs were crate trained as babies, but none of them have been in a crate since they were old enough to not potty or destroy anything in the house.

We just use the crate long enough to teach them how to properly behave in the house and potty train them, and then you can ween them off it as they get older and give them more freedom to stay out!

4. It is a valuable life skill!

What happens if you are hospitalized, or your dog must stay at the vet overnight, or you need to fly with your dog, but they have never been in a kennel before? Odds are your dog is going to freak out WAY more than usual because now not only are they in a new location and separated from you, but they are being forced into a small box for the first time in their life. So, teaching them how to be okay in a crate is setting both you and them up for success in case of an emergency!

THINGS TO AVOID WHILE CRATE TRAINING.

1. Never use your dogs' crate as a punishment!

This is their space, do not ruin it with your temper. They should never be yelled at immediately prior to going in, shoved into it, or yelled at while they are in there. While most of this seems self-explanatory, you would be surprised at how many people make one of those mistakes!

2. Make sure you are using the right sized crate!

A dog will not go to the bathroom in the same space they sleep in, which will aid in potty training. However, if you use too big of a crate, they can section it off, using half to sleep and half to potty if necessary. You want to use a crate that is big enough for them to stand up, lay down, and move around comfortably in, but not large enough for them to be able to section it off. If you have a large breed dog, you should expect to go through multiple crates or consider buying one that has an ajustable divider. The crate should fit the size of the dog currently, not what they will be ehrn they are full grown.

3. Make it as positive as possible.

Whether you use something that smells like their mom and litter mates, or a warm water bottle, or even a stuffed animal, make it comfortable! Remember, we want our dogs to love their crates as much as you love climbing in your bed at the end of the night, so make it enjoyable!

4. Don't leave them in there for too long periods.

The longest your dog should ever be in the kennel is at nighttime when you are sleeping, and even then, if they whine like they need to go potty, you need to take them out. Otherwise, if you work full time and they must be in the kennel, you should either schedule your lunch break in a way that you can go home to let them out or find another way of making this happen through a dog sitter, friend, or even taking them to daycare. If your dog spends too much time in their kennel, eventually, they will become obstinate about it and not want to go in.

5. Keep your kids out of the kennel.

As cute as it is to see your kids and puppy playing together, there are tons of opportunities for this to happen without letting your kid crawl inside their kennel with them. Let the kennel be the dog's space and the dog's space alone. Kids can be overwhelming for some dogs, so giving them a chance to even get away from you and your kids can help prevent any guarding or aggressive behaviors in the future.

COMMON QUESTIONS:

1. What if my dog is older and has issues with barrier aggression or crate reactivity?

This is a relatively common issue, especially with dogs who come from a shelter or those who were never properly introduced to a crate at a young age. The good news is, there are some really easy ways that we can work on barrier aggression and help our dogs feel more secure going into them.

2. What are crate games:

Crate games are exercises we use with dogs of all ages to make going into their crate fun and rewarding.

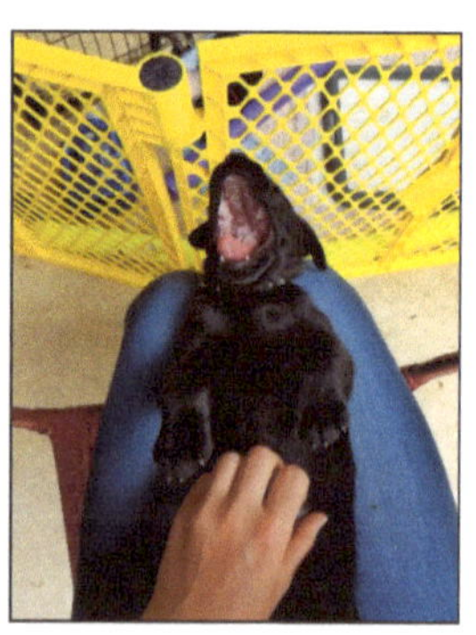

Not only does it teach them that going into it is rewarding, but that going into the crate does not always mean they are going to be stuck in there for long periods of time, so there is no reason to fight it!

3. If I am using the crate to help control unwanted behaviors, how is it not a form of punishment?

When we are talking about not using the crate as a form of punishment, we mean that the puppy should not be yelled at or scolded while they are in the kennel, nor should they be thrown into it out of anger because of something they have done. Rather, by calmly putting our puppy into the kennel at the right time, we are teaching them how to calm down and soothe themselves on their own.

Remember, an overly tired puppy will start to act out just like a toddler would, so most of the time, they need time to rest and reset, which will be hard to do if they still can run freely and interact with you. Think of it more as putting them down for a much-needed nap.

POTTY TRAINING MADE EASY(ER)

Potty training is one part of owning a puppy that everyone dreads because let's be honest, no one likes having a puppy piddle in their house. So, I am going to give you a quick how-to guide to make your next potty-training endeavor as quick and pain-free as possible, as well as some things to avoid while you are trying to do it.

HOW TO POTTY TRAIN YOUR PUPPY:

1. Decide on a schedule as to when your puppy is going to eat, get most of their exercise, and go to bed.

Puppies' potty habits are predictable, so the more regimented their schedule is the better. A good rule of thumb is that anytime your puppy eats, drinks, wakes up from a nap, or is playing and then stops suddenly, they will probably have to go to the bathroom. Therefore, by putting them on a schedule you will better be able to predict their bathroom habits and prevent unnecessary accidents in the house.

2. Put everything on cue and create a pattern.

A sample pattern might look like this:

- Puppy displays a sign that they might need to go outside (sniffing the ground, circling)
- You say, "let's go outside."
- Pick the puppy up and walk them outside, then put them down exactly where you want them to relieve themselves and say, "go potty."
- By picking them up we are ensuring that they will not be able to potty in the house on the way out, and it allows the owner to designate specific areas of the yard that they might want the dog to relieve themselves in.
- Stay outside and wait to see the puppy go to the bathroom - this will allow you to not only verify that they relieved themselves, preventing any accidents upon coming inside, but reward them for going potty when they do.

Another mistake a lot of owners make is putting their puppy outside and assuming they know what to do or that they went, only to bring them back inside and have them go, but consider this: if no one taught you how to go to the bathroom using the toilet, would you know how?

- Once the puppy has finished relieving themselves say "good potty" and reward them heavily.
- Make sure that you do not interrupt the puppy while they are in the middle of going to the bathroom, as the excitement can cause them to stop prematurely out of excitement, especially with male dogs, increasing the likelihood that they will finish in the house when you go inside.
- If you take them outside and they do not go to the bathroom, do not come inside, and allow them to run the house freely. Instead, put them in their crate, wait 10 minutes, and then try the process over again.
- By keeping them confined we are guaranteeing that they are not running off into the house to relieve themselves somewhere that they shouldn't.

- Be consistent! The more you can reward positive potty habits in the beginning the faster and easier it will be to potty train your pup!

3. Do not overestimate the amount of time your puppy can hold their bladder.

It is always better to take them out more frequently and be able to reward them for going potty, than it is for them to have an accident in the house.

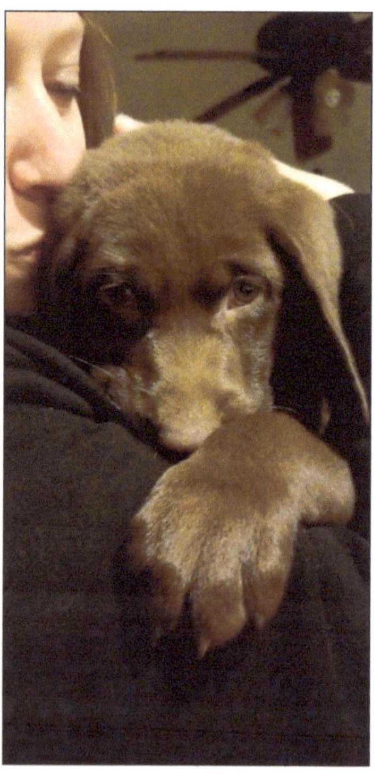

4. If your dog has an accident in the house, punishing them after the fact is not going to do anything other than make them fear going to the bathroom in front of you.

Dogs are associative learners, so when you try to punish them after the fact, they do not associate the punishment with going in the wrong location, only that they went. In turn, your dog will be less likely to relieve themselves in front of you, even outside when we want them to. If you catch them while they are still in the act of going or about to go, say "NO", pick them up, and start your cuing process as you get them outside, and then reward them for finishing outside. Now we have made a negative association with going inside the house, while simultaneously making a positive association with them going potty in the appropriate place.

5. NEVER teach your dog that going inside the house inside for any reason is okay.

One of the biggest mistakes I see people make is using puppy pads to try and potty train their dogs inside the house. Dogs will not associate going to the bathroom on the potty pad inside with going to the bathroom outside. It is a totally different surface, environment, and experience, so you will have to completely break the behavior of going inside on the potty pad and re-train them to go outside. Unless you are prepared to have your dog potty inside your house for the rest of their life, do not make potty pads a viable option for them.

Additionally, I will always give clients the chance to sit down and construct a potty plan with me that will work for them. Often, people struggle with changing their habits, but do very well in a routine, especially if there is someone else telling them to do it. Therefore, if I can help them establish that routine, they are much more likely to be successful.

6. Here is an example of a potty-training schedule for a client who works 8 hours a day:

- 6am: Wake up, take the puppy outside immediately to potty and allow a few extra minutes outside to let them run around after they have done so. If your puppy does not go immediately, do not bring them back inside and be patient. After being in the kennel all night, they will have to go.
- 6:15-6:45am: Allow the puppy to stay with you in a supervised setting while you start to get ready. We want to ensure that we are keeping an eye on them in case they start displaying "I need to go outside" behaviors so that we can take them outside if necessary.
- 6:45-7am: Take the puppy outside again and allow them the chance to try and potty. Most likely, after playing for a while they will have to pee again.
- 7-7:15am: Feed the puppy their first meal of the day. Once they have finished eating, immediately take them outside again to see if they must go poop.
- 7:15-7:45am: Allow the puppy to have a few more minutes of supervised play time, whether this is inside or outside. Remember, the puppy is about to be in the crate for a while, so the more exercise they get in the morning, the better. If you

choose to stay outside, try to ensure that they go to the bathroom before you bring them in for the last time. If you come back inside, make sure that you take them out one more time before putting them in the crate for the day.

- 7:45am: Put the puppy in the crate for the day, ensuring that they have something to do while they are in there, such as a filled and frozen Kong, chew bone, or other form of mental stimulation.

LEAVE FOR WORK

- 11:45/12: Either you or a pet sitter/walker should come and let them out to walk, play, and potty. Depending on how long you (the sitter) are there, take the puppy out to potty, on a walk or play a short game of tug/fetch, and then to potty one more time after the walk/play time before putting them back into their kennel with another form of mental stimulation.
- 4PM: Come home from work, immediately take the puppy outside to potty.
- 4:15PM: Take the puppy for a walk or provide play time. Just make sure that they have emptied their system before coming back inside.
- 5-5:15PM: Feed the puppy their dinner.
- 5:30PM: Take the puppy outside to potty, as they will likely have to after eating dinner.
- 5:45-9:45PM: This should be supervised time in the house, as well as time to do some training and spend quality time with

them. Be sure to watch for any signs that the puppy might have to use the bathroom. If they start showing signs of having to go to the bathroom at any time, be sure to get them outside right away so they can be rewarded for going to the right place. At no point during this big window should the puppy be unsupervised, and if possible, in their crate, as this can cause them to start not wanting to go in their crate if they are in it too much.

- 10PM: Take the puppy out for the last time, put them in their crate for bed.

SITTING AND WAITING FOR THEIR FOOD BOWL

Have you ever tried to give your dog food or water only for them to jump up and spill whatever it is you are holding? It can be frustrating to say the least, and nobody wants to have a negative association with mealtime! That is why I teach all my dogs to sit and wait for their food and water bowls. Not only does it give me the chance to get everything situated without them all over me, but it teaches them to control their excitement and build some fundamental training skills. Remember, one of the things that young dogs struggle with the most is patience and impulse control, so what better way to start helping them learn these important skills than making them work for their food!

HOW TO TEACH IT:

1. Prepare your dog's food on the counter, away from where they can reach you.
2. Take their food bowl and use it as a lure to get them to sit and then tell them to wait.
3. Slowly start lowering the food bowl to the ground in front of them. If at any point the dog pops up out of the sit, give them the no reward marker, and raise it backup. Hopefully, the dog

will automatically sit back down, but if they don't, put them back into the sit and start the process over.

4. Once the dog can stay in the sitting position while the food bowl is lowered all the way to the ground, release them to come and eat. Sometimes, at the very beginning of training if I have a pup that is struggling, I will release them as I am setting the bowl down. Then, as they get better and better, I will add duration to their wait after it is already on the ground. Trying to add duration to this exercise too soon is only going to end up with the puppy getting frustrated as they won't understand right away what it is you are expecting from them, and sometimes need to be rewarded for smaller steps along the way.

5. As the puppy is eating, this is also a great time for you to work with them and being comfortable with people around their food. Stay there, pet them, talk softly to them, and even continue to place a small amount of food into their bowl while they are eating. If the dog doesn't seem bothered with any of this, you can also use this chance to work food bowl exchange exercises. You can do this by slowly picking up their food bowl, giving them a treat in exchange for the food bowl, and then setting it back down on the ground. Again, this is just a good exercise to do to get the dog comfortable with people being close to their food bowl, or even moving their food bowl, while still knowing that it is going to be rewarding to them regardless. This is especially good exercise for anyone who has kids at home!

THINGS TO AVOID:

1. Never withhold their food from them if they are not able to do it right away.

Normally, with a little patience, dogs will pick up this exercise quickly. However, some dogs are going to struggle and will need to be rewarded for smaller steps along the way. If you have a dog that is really struggling to pick it up, it would be better to teach them leave-it first, that way you can incorporate it into the exercise as you are lowering it to the ground.

2. Do not yell at your dog while it is eating, or trying to eat, as this will likely make them feel as though they need to protect their food from you, which we do not want.

Even if they didn't get it quite right, or break a little earlier than anticipated, you never want your dog to feel like they must fight to be fed.

3. If you have a dog who is food aggressive, you should work on that first before trying this exercise.

Here are a couple ways that you can start working on food aggression in dogs:

- Hand feed the dog as much as possible. This will teach them that the only way they are going to get food is if it is from you, and that acting aggressively about it is not going to get them anywhere.
- After they are willing to eat from your hand with no issues, either sit with their food bowl between your legs on the floor or hold it in your lap. Then, slowly put the food into their bowl one handful at a time. This way, we are continuing the association that their food comes from your hand, and they will get used to your hand still being there even with the bowl involved.
- Once they are okay with that exercise while you are sitting still, progress it to a standing position. Continue talking nicely to

them, petting them as necessary, and putting the food into their bowl slowly as you move freely around them. There is a big difference between sitting with them and standing over them, so don't be surprised if they are a little more hesitant to trust you at first.

- When the dog gets to the point that you can move around them freely while putting food into their bowl, you should be okay to start working on them waiting for their food bowl. By this point, they should understand that they do not have to fight for or defend their food and that will make them much more accepting of the food bowl exercise.

NO JUMPING FROM THE GET-GO

ONE OF THE MOST COMMON PROBLEMS PEOPLE BRING TO ME IS their dog jumping on them or other people. So, today I am going to give you a couple tips and tricks I have used in the past to teach dogs not to jump.

Please know I am not going to be talking about strictly teaching a place cue or teaching them alternate behaviors in general. The reason for this is because a lot of people will not put in the time and effort on their own to work on more advanced skills, but that doesn't mean that jumping doesn't need to stop as it can result in someone getting hurt!

Therefore, I am going to start with the most positive form of training, and then work our way down. This way, if you have already tried one mode and were unsuccessful, you can try another one that will hopefully work for you!

Tip 1:Be consistent from the time you bring them home:

Remember, if you do not want your 90lb full grown dog jumping on you, then don't let your 9lb puppy do it either.

Dogs are not aware that they are huge. All they know is that jumping on you to get attention as a puppy worked, so jumping on you as an adult has got to work too!!

Always greet your puppy low and reward them for keeping all four feet on the ground. If they never have the chance to jump on you, then it will never become rewarding for them.

If your puppy does try to jump on you, give them the no-reward marker and back away from them. If they do anything other than jump, reward them heavily, even if they are just standing and looking at you!

Often, if a puppy sees that jumping on you does not work or is never given the opportunity to do so, they will give up and sit, which is a great way to show them that sitting is going to be what gets them rewarded.

Tip 2: Turn your back or ignore them when they jump on you, and only offer them attention or praise when they sit or keep all four feet on the ground:

Dogs jump on us because they are trying to get our attention, so if you ignore it and only pay attention to them when they offer good behavior, good behavior is just as rewarding! If you do turn your back and they continue to jump on you, try to give them the no-reward marker and then praise them if they decide to sit or just quit jumping and keep all their feet on the floor.

Many people think that by giving them the no-reward marker that we are acknowledging it and making it rewarding for them, but if they are still jumping when your attention is removed then they either do not know why you are ignoring them, or do not yet know the alternative behavior you want them to do. Therefore, by giving the no reward marker, we are asking them to try something different, and then rewarding them when they do.

Tip 3:Greet dogs with your hands low, slip a thumb through their collar so you can hold them down and off you, and reward them for keeping all four paws on the ground:

When you get home, get to a friend's house, or whatever the case may be, dogs are excited to see you. Now, you have the ability to "help" the dog keep all four paws planted on the ground while simultaneously rewarding them for good behavior!

Tip 4:Use their leashes to help! If you know people are coming over to your house and you don't want your dog jumping all over them, start by putting their leash on and letting them drag it around the house:

Then, when a guest comes over, step on the portion of the leash that is lying on the ground. The dog is unaware that it is the leash holding them down, just that they are no longer able to jump up. Now, you have an easy way to greet your guests and allow them to greet your dog without having to worry about them jumping around all crazy and potentially hurting someone else or themselves. Or you can always use it to lead the dog away, and then re-approach once they have calmed down a little. This is very similar to the U-turn training we discussed in the exposure section.

Tip 5: Put them behind a baby gate 5-10 feet from the door so they are not able to get to guests right away, and then guests can greet them through the gate by asking them for a sit:

This way, we are removing their ability to jump on people altogether, but still allowing them the opportunity to say hello in a controlled environment. Plus, then if they are so hyped up that they can't calm down for a second or two, you know that they are still not able to reinforce the jumping behavior and you can reward them for something nice.

Tip 6:If rewarding an alternate behavior does not help, nor do any of the options above, then you may have to resort to positive punishment, especially if the dog is hurting its owners or other people:

The first thing to try would be putting your knee up when they try to jump up on you, which will not only keep you safe, but make the jumping behavior un-rewarding for the dog.

After you put your knee up, if the dog backs off and offers you a calm behavior, still be sure to reward them for it.

Another option would be to use an e-collar on the beep setting. This way, if you see your dog approaching someone looking like they are going to jump, you can use the beep to get their attention back on you, and then ask them for a calm behavior, or at least give you the opportunity to get them back under control. If the beep does not work then you can increase the stimulation, but before you do this, you need to make sure that they understand what it is you want them to do.

YOU SHOULD NEVER USE AN E-COLLAR ON A DOG WHO DOES NOT KNOW WHAT THEY ARE BEING CORRECTED FOR, OTHERWISE, YOU ARE JUST ABUSING THEM WITHOUT TEACHING THEM ANYTHING!

CHEWING

Do you have problems with your dog chewing up things they shouldn't? Are you frustrated because they are destroying things in your house when you are providing them with appropriate toys and chews? To really understand why your dog is chewing things they shouldn't, we will first examine the WHY behind the behavior.

Chewing is an extremely natural behavior for dogs and a crucial part of their ability to maintain teeth and gum health as they age.

Puppies use it to massage their sore gums as they lose their baby teeth, and again to ensure that their adult teeth are properly impacted in their gums.

Adult dogs use chewing to not only maintain the integrity of their teeth, but to keep their teeth clean and their gums healthy. It is also an amazing stress relief activity and a great way to wear down your pup when physical exercise isn't an option.

Therefore, it is important that as we work with our dogs on "problem chewing" that we focus more on encouraging appropriate chewing and less on punishing bad chewing.

How to stop problem chewing while encouraging good chewing:

1. Never reprimand your dog for chewing something bad without replacing it with something it should be chewing on:

For example, if you catch your dog chewing on the leg of your table and you reprimand them, all you have taught them is that they should not chew AT ALL. However, if you tell them "No" for chewing the leg of the table, but then immediately give them a meaty bone, you have taught them that while they shouldn't chew on the table, they SHOULD chew on the bone.

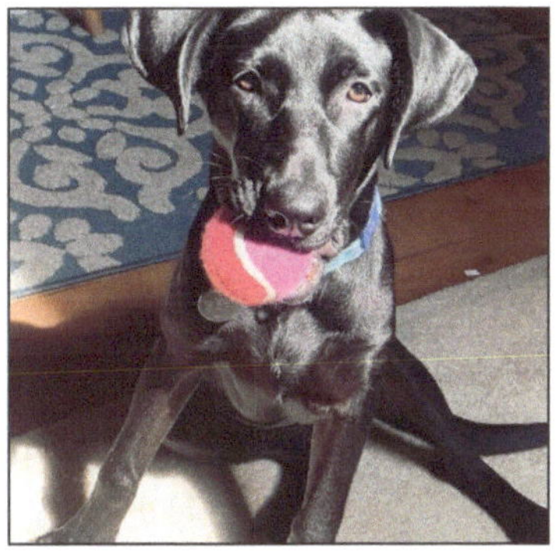

2. Try to avoid giving your dog toys that closely resemble household items:

For example, if you have a dog that likes to tear up pillows or eat socks, you should not promote the destruction of toys of similar nature. Dogs are associative learners, and they often struggle to tell the difference between a toy that is OKAY to be destroyed, and a pillow or stuffed animal that is not.

3. Choose high reward bones and chews:

If you want your dog to be more interested in bones and chews than they are on, say your shoes, then you must give them bones and chews that are more interesting than your shoes. For example, I only give my dogs raw meaty bones and "stinky treats", that way everything else they come across is less enticing while also ensuring that they won't be ingesting something that they shouldn't.

4. Do not leave your dog unsupervised:

Just like with potty training, if you are not confident in your dog's ability to be left alone without being destructive, then leave them crated or in a gated area with an appropriate chew toy when they are unsupervised. This will guarantee that they will not be able to go off and chew something they shouldn't while allowing you to promote the chewing of good objects.

5. Do not rely on deterrents to keep your dog from chewing:

While these can be beneficial tools, they do not have the ability to tell your dog what is appropriate for them to chew on. Therefore, if you are going to use deterrents, make sure that they are still being used in combination with everything I mentioned above to ensure that we are not just telling them what they cannot do, but also what they can.

When you break chewing down it is a simple behavior to conquer and modify. Remember, it's not about discouraging chewing, but encouraging proper and healthy chewing!

SECTION THREE:
TEACHING THE OBEDIENCE CUES

BUILDING THE ASSOCIATION BETWEEN OUR MARKER AND FOOD TREAT

WHY TEACH IT?

THE VERY FIRST THING WE WANT TO TEACH OUR DOGS WHEN we start training is their mark word or clicker association to a food treat, so that we have the ability to tell our dogs exactly when they have performed the behavior we are asking them to do. Without building this association, you would have to put the treat in their mouth the exact moment they do the behavior, which will be very difficult and even slow down the training process.

TRAINER TIP!

Many trainers believe that the clicker is easier to build an association with because it sounds the same every time and is a distinct sound that is easy for the dog to pick up on. However, I have always favored mark-words for two reasons. First, I have seen clients get very out of sorts when they show up to train and have forgotten their clicker, and they believe that they will not be able to train their dog without it. So, I never want clients to feel like they MUST have a clicker to be able to communicate with their dogs properly. Second, many people who are inexperienced with dog training have a hard time managing a dog, leash, treats, and a clicker simultaneously, while still being able to mark and reward at the appropriate time. Therefore, I never try to steer people one way or the other and I let them decide what they think will be easiest, and most successful for them.

HOW TO TEACH IT

To build an association, the first thing you will have to decide is if you are going to be using a clicker or a mark-word. If you are choosing to use a mark-word, you want to make sure that it is something you do not already use a lot daily, and that it is short and easy to say the same way each time. For the sake of ease, whether you choose a mark word or use the clicker, we will refer to them as "markers" from here on out.

First, we are going to put our dog on a leash so they cannot wander away from us and get a handful of treats. Then, we will give them our marker, and immediately give them a food treat. You will continue doing this until the dog looks at you expecting the treat immediately following the marker, and this is when you will know that you have properly built an association. ("Yes" -> dog immediately looks for the treat to come)

In other words, the dog has now learned that when they hear that marker, a food treat is going to follow. Not only does this allow us to tell them that they did the right thing, but it allows for some leniency in the timing of the delivery of the food treat, since they already know that a treat is coming no matter what.

TEACHING THEM THEIR NAME.

WHY TEACH IT?

Now that we have built an association with our marker and a reward, the next thing we want to ensure is that our dog knows their name. Remember, dogs, just like kids, must be taught what their name is. Just because you say it to them regularly does not necessarily mean that they have associated it with themselves, and this often leads people to believe that the dog is ignoring them, when in fact they just didn't know that you were talking to them. This also results in the owner saying the dog's name over and over and over until they finally respond, which teaches the dog that they don't have to respond the first, second, or even third time, but if they respond eventually, they will be okay. Therefore, we are going to save ourselves a lot of time and hassle by not only teaching them their name, but that they should respond the first time, every time.

TRAINER TIP!

There are so many instances when I use the dog's name as a preemptory cue, so they know I need their attention, and that something is going to follow, much the same way most people use a focus cue. However, since there are so many instances when I am working with multiple dogs at the same time, I like to ensure that I can get the focus of an individual dog, and I am not the type of trainer that likes to have "unnecessary steps" in my cueing. For example, if I was to use a focus cue instead, it would be "Hershey, Focus, (additional cueing)", whereas I teach all the dogs I work with that when I say their name alone, they need to stop and give me their attention. As a trainer, you can decide what and how you would like to do this. If you want to teach their name and a focus cue, that is fine, and you can teach the focus cue the same way that you would teach them their name!

HOW TO TEACH IT

To teach their name, we will start by saying their name once in a high-pitched and fun way, and then wait for them to look at us. We will do this by taking out a treat, showing it to them, and then holding it out beside our heads bringing their attention up towards our face. We will say their name once in a high-pitched and excited tone, and then wait to see them shift their eyes from the treat to your eyes. The second that your dog looks at you, you will give them your marker and reward  them. Remember, we need to be precise with our marker here, because we want to mark the exact second our dog looks at us and we know that we have their attention.

While we are working on this it is important that we are patient and give them time to respond without saying their name multiple times. If we just start repeating their name over and over, and then still reward them when they look at us, they will learn that they do not have to respond the first time, every time, and that if they respond eventually, they will still get rewarded. So patience is key here.

Once your dog is to the point where they no longer must be lured to look up at you, and are responding to their name immediately, the first time, you will know that you have now successfully taught them their name.

Generally, if I am working with a brand-new dog or a young dog/puppy, I will use their name as a warm-up exercise over the next couple of lessons. Not only does it help to reinforce the fact that they are going to get rewarded each time we call them, but it is a great way to get them into "working mode" and have their attention on you before you start working on the harder elements. Additionally, it is an excellent way to start working on the recall, since a lot of dogs will get into the habit of coming to you for a reward once they learn that their name is rewarding for them.

THE NO-REWARD MARKER

WHY TEACH IT?

A no-reward marker is used to tell our dogs that they didn't quite complete the behavior we were asking for, and that we would like them to do something else, so we can reward them. Just like being able to tell them that they did something correctly, it's equally important that we can communicate that they did something incorrectly, as this is going to keep them from getting frustrated during their training sessions. As with any other situation in life, how can you correct something if you never know that what you're doing is wrong? Therefore, we want to eliminate this confusion from the equation entirely and can do so by using a no-reward marker.

TRAINER TIP!

I do not use the word "No" as a no-reward marker because I use it for a separate reason. When I use a no-reward marker, I am not trying to punish the dog or get them to stop what they are doing entirely. I am simply trying to communicate that I do not like what they are doing, and that I would like them to offer me something else so I can reward them. Your no-reward marker should always result in you rewarding the dog in one way or another. However, when I use the word "No", I use it to tell them to stop whatever it is they are doing immediately and look at me. While many people say this is a "punishment", there are certain situations where dogs need to stop what they are doing for their safety, and sometimes the safety of others, and it is important that we have a way to just make them stop and redirect. This is when I use "No."

HOW TO TEACH IT

Your no-reward marker, just like your marker, should be something that you don't say regularly, and something that feels natural. For me, I say "eh-eh", but you are welcome to use anything that works for you.

To teach the no-reward marker, we are going to start with our dogs on a leash and have a couple treats in our hands. Then, you will toss one of the treats on the ground in front of your dog, but not close enough that they are able to get to it at the end of the leash. As soon as you see them go after it, you will give them the no-reward marker and wait for them to redirect. The second that they disengage from the treat on the ground, even if just for a moment, you will mark and reward. Even after the dog has disengaged and got the treat from you, DO NOT let them get the treat that is on the ground, but rather, either throw another treat, or allow them to go after the same one again. Not only will this help reinforce the no-reward marker faster, but it will make it much easier to teach them to leave-it later since they have already been taught to disengage and redirect to us.

If you have given the no-reward marker and they are not responding, start slowly walking backwards, applying light and gradual pressure on the leash, while vocally encouraging your pup to turn back towards you by using sounds like "hey, hey" or kissing noises. As soon as they turn and redirect to you, mark, and reward. Remember, we are not yanking or pulling them, we are just applying enough pressure to get them to want to look in our direction.

You will continue this process until they redirect to you immediately following the no-reward marker, and there is no need for you to apply any pressure to their collar. Then you will know that you have correctly taught the no-reward marker.

SIT

WHY TEACH IT?

Now we are going to move onto what I believe is one of the easiest things to teach our dogs to sit.

While this behavior is simple to teach, it is a great behavior for dogs to learn since it gives us a neutral position to put them in and keep them calm when they are meeting new people, getting their leash put on, waiting for their food bowls and so much more. In other words, it is a comfortable and natural position that we can put our dogs in when all we need is for them to be still for a couple moments.

TRAINER TIP!

One thing I like to do when I am teaching obedience cues is start tying the cue in almost immediately, but following the completion of the exercise by marking, rewarding, and then saying, "good sit." You do NOT have to do this; I have just found that it helps the dog start associating the cue with the behavior they just performed. This way, even if you mess up and cue them early on during the association stage, it will make it less likely that they are going to ignore the cue since they have already started building a basic association with it. Additionally, it will make it much easier to tie the cue in when you are ready.

HOW TO TEACH IT

We are going to teach our dogs to sit by using the lure method. You will put the treat directly in front of their nose, so they are able to smell it, but not take it from you, and then slowly move it up and over their heads towards their backend.

As their head follows the treat, their butt will have no choice but to lower down to the ground. The moment your dog's butt touches the ground, you will mark and reward this behavior. For right now, do not worry if they pop right back up, as we will start building that duration next.

If you are having trouble getting your dog to sit using the lure because they just keep moving backwards, there is another way you can try. Take your lure and put it on the dog's nose and get them to take a couple of steps towards you. Then, take your lure and bring it up doing the scooping method while simultaneously ensuring that you are standing tall with your shoulders back, and stepping slightly into the dog's space.

Dogs operate a lot on the premise of respect, so if we have a more commanding presence, they will automatically want to pay more attention to us. So, as we move slowly into their space, they will continue to lift their heads to give us that attention, making their butts drop towards the ground.

Another option would be to wait for the dog to offer it naturally, and then mark and reward the behavior. This is called capturing behavior, and it can be another great way to teach obedience cues. Many dogs will offer a sit naturally, so we can capitalize on this by marking, rewarding, and saying "good sit." Once you have successfully captured the behavior about 5 times, go ahead and try the lure method again, since they already have an idea of what is going to get them rewarded and they are more likely to respond.

Once you have found the method that works best for you, continue luring them until you know that they are going to sit every time, and then you will slowly start fading the lure and tying in your verbal cue. As you are fading the lure, this is also a really good time to add in a hand signal if you choose, which will allow you to ask your dog to sit without a verbal cue. For me, I like to take the treat and do a kind of scooping motion above their head and stop there, which gives the illusion of the treat still going up and over (like your lure would). Slowly, I will keep it closer to me and further from them, fading the lure and creating my hand signal simultaneously.

Once the dog is responding to the verbal cue and hand signal alone, we will start working on their duration, as it is hard to add distance or distraction if they can't keep their butts planted. To do this, we will ask them to sit, mark (do not give food treat, just marker), wait 2 seconds, give food treat and release. What this is going to do is start teaching the dog that when we put them in the sit, they need to stay seated until they are rewarded and released, even if it isn't immediately.

You will continue this exercise by gradually adding more and more time between when you mark and reward the behavior until they are able to hold that sit for 5-10 seconds.

As with all obedience cues, it is important that you are working on your sit in as many different locations as you can. Because dogs are associative learners, I would say that they need to learn the same thing in at least 6 different locations before they truly associate the behavior with every location and not just home. For example, have you ever heard someone say, "he doesn't do this at home, I don't understand?!" Well, this is because they have not taken the time to work with their dogs in multiple locations, therefore, the dog does not associate those behaviors in general, but rather, only in your house where most of the training as taken place.

When you first start working on your cues in a new location, don't be surprised if you must take a step back and lure them a couple of times to ensure that they are going to be responsive. There are going to be new places, people, and things all around them, so it is important that we set them up for success. Remember, it is always better to take a step backwards than it is to give them your cue and have them ignore it, as this will only teach them that they don't have to listen and creates more work for you later.

STAY

WHY TEACH IT?

WHILE ALL OBEDIENCE CUES WE TEACH HAVE A PURPOSE AND meaning behind them, the next three are probably the most important as they could be vital in one day saving your dog's life. Whether you need them to stay put while you cross a busy street to get the mail or need to keep them from getting even closer to something dangerous while you remove it, having a strong stay can be instrumental in a dog's safety. Not to mention, it can set you up for success in a lot of follow on trick movements and advanced training scenarios, and who doesn't want their dog to be able to do cool stuff?

TRAINER TIP!

The stay can be hard to teach, especially with very energetic, enthusiastic, or reward driven dogs. Therefore, it is always better to move extremely slowly at first so they can be rewarded for staying a plethora of times before you start adding too much of your own movement. If you try to move too quickly and the dog fails too many times right off the bat, it is going to be extremely difficult to backtrack and teach them what it is we want. So, if what we want is for them to stay in one spot until either we return to them or release them, then we need to be able to build that exact association with our stay right from the beginning. However, if they are successful at the beginning and can understand what is expected from the stay cue, it will be very easy to increase that stay and solidify it faster.

Additionally, in my opinion, unless you are trying to train your dog to do advanced obedience, or trials, or something of that nature, if the dog changes their position, but not their location, I consider that a successful stay. For example, if I put a dog in a sit stay and leave them there for a couple minutes, and they decide to lay down and get comfortable, I am still going to reward them as long as they didn't wander off to do so. Why? Because when I say stay, I am worried about their location, not so much about what their body posture is. Therefore, if they would rather lie down than sit, so be it, if they stay put. As I said, this is just my opinion, and this does not apply to those dogs whom you are training for competition purposes, but rather the everyday pup who has every right to be comfortable as you do.

HOW TO TEACH IT

To teach stay, first you will have to decide what position you want your dog to start in. You are welcome to put them in either the sit or the down, but I would recommend choosing whichever one they have already built the most duration in, as they are less likely to get up in the beginning stages of learning this cue. However, a good rule of thumb is this: the more contact their body has with the ground, the less likely they are to get up and follow you. For example, staying from the moving position is the hardest to achieve while an extended stay in the down is the simplest.

Once they are in either the sit or the down, we are going to start with our feet staggered, and then put our hand in front of their face like a stop sign and give them the "stay" cue. Unlike many of the other cues we teach, stay must be introduced right at the beginning as we are signaling to the dog that our movement is coming, and that they should not follow. Then, lean slightly backwards away from them, introducing basic upper body movement away from the dog, and if they do not move, we will come right back, mark and reward them for staying. This entire process should not take more than a couple of seconds, so do not try to stay away from your dog for too long.

Remember, when we are teaching the stay at the beginning, we always want to come back to our dogs to reward them, as the number one reason they will break it is to try and follow you to see where you are going. So, if they learn right off the bat that we are always going to come back to them, they will not feel the need to break their stay early and follow you, but rather associate the stay with waiting until your return.

After we have done the lean back several times and they have an idea of what we are doing, we will slowly start adding in steps backwards away from them. We will only be adding one step at a time, and then coming back to reward them each time. You will want to work up to 5-7 steps away, while slightly varying your angles away from them introducing lateral movements, and then we will start working on moving around them.

As we start making our circle around them, there are a few keys to making sure that your dog is successful. First, you need to ensure that you are keeping a close eye on your pup as you start working your way around them. This way, if they start to pop out of it, you can stop right where you are, reward them for staying up to that point, and then re-cue them and keep working your way around them. Keep in mind, the point that most dogs will break is when you are almost all the way behind them, and it is time for them to change the direction they are looking at you. Once they have done it, they will realize they can turn their heads to see you on the other side, but at first, a lot of dogs will try to get up so they can follow you as you move behind them.) It is always better to stop and reward them for the stay they have completed so far than it is to allow them to break it and not get rewarded at all, as this is what will lead to frustration and degradation of your stay cue. However, after several attempts like this, you should be able to walk a complete circle around them.

Generally, once your dog allows you to make circles around them without popping up, the stay cue is very easy to make stronger and stronger. This is when I will focus on longer and longer durations, then adding further distances, and then finally distractions, such as rolling balls around them.

COME

WHY TEACH IT?

Today we are going to be working on our dogs' recalls, which is one of the most important cues you will ever teach your dog. Not only will this give us the ability to have our dogs come to us when we need them to, but it is vital for keeping them safe in many different scenarios, especially if you have the dream of being able to trust your dog off-leash.

Something vitally important to keep in mind when we are working on recall, is that we want it to be fun and exciting for the dog. In a lot of situations, we will be asking them to come away from something that is rewarding for them such as ending play time, calling them away from something they want to chase, or even putting them in their crate so we can leave.

Therefore, it is extremely important that the dog learns that recall is always going to be more rewarding to them than whatever it is we are recalling them away from. If your dog's tail isn't wagging each time they come to you, then odds are, you have not made it fun enough!

TRAINER TIP!

When I am teaching recall, I have a zero-tolerance policy for them not coming. If I try to recall them once and they do not come, I will try to use my body movements and high-pitched noises (excited and erratic) to try to entice them, and if that fails, I will walk over and get them. I am not punishing them for not coming, as this might make them fearful of coming to me period, but I will never allow them to ignore me all together, as this is only teaching them that recall is optional, which it isn't. Additionally, this is the only basic obedience cue that I ever use an e-collar with, especially when I am adding distance and distraction to it. I still do not shock them unless I am sure that they know what I am asking for and know that they are choosing to ignore me, but I will use the beep setting to break their attention on whatever they are fixated on. Then, I start my excited body movements and sounds to get them to come back to me and reward them heavily for doing so.

HOW TO TEACH IT

Unlike many of the other basic obedience cues, we will not be using the lure for this exercise, but rather we will be using our body movements and high-pitched fun noises to entice them to come to us, and then reward them heavily when they do so. By body movements, I mean moving quickly away from them (initiating a chase), clapping, patting on the ground, and even moving my hands around in front of me in an erratic behavior, all of which will entice them to want to chase me the way they would prey, only to be rewarded once they get there.

Now, since we have already taken the time to teach them their name and solidify it, we are going to use that as an attention getter and preparatory command to let our dogs know that we need their attention, and that something else is going to follow. So, the first thing we are going to do is either have them on a long leash or in a confined area that they are not able to get out of, with as minimal distractions as possible. Please note that even at the very beginning of training, if your goal is to have a good dog off-leash, then you should try to work them off-leash as much as possible. No matter what anyone says, many dogs are too smart to be fooled by a leash dragging on the ground behind them, and they will quickly learn that as soon as that leash goes away, so does your control of the situation.

Plus, there are very few situations where we will NEED our recall while they are on a leash. Therefore, I always recommend working recall off-leash as much as possible if the dog is in a controlled environment. Then, we are going to toss a treat out onto the floor and allow them to go get it. As soon as they get the treat, we are going to say their name in a high-pitched and excited tone, and then start using our excited body movements and sounds to get their attention back to us.

This should entice the puppy to want to "chase" you, and when they start running towards you, present the treat down low and continue encouraging them. As soon as they get all the way to you, mark and give the reward, and say, "good come!"

Remember, rewarding a dog for recall means that we are rewarding them for coming all the way back to us so we can get them back under control, not in the near vicinity of us so we must spend 5 more minutes trying to convince them to get close enough so we can restrain them. Therefore, we will NEVER reward the dog unless they come all the way back to our hands. Generally, because dogs are so people orientated, once they figure out what will get them rewarded, this isn't too difficult. However, those older "stubborn" dogs and even fearful dogs might not want to in the beginning, which is why it is vital we only reward the correct behaviors, and we make it super rewarding for them.

Another way to make recall fun for your dog is by playing the "puppy puppy" game either at home or with someone else the dog trusts. Again, we will set the dog up for success by being in a low stimulation setting and having some high reward treats. Then, you will have one person on one side of the room, with the other person and the dog on the other. Now, you will take turns calling the dog back and forth using the described method above, ensuring to reward them heavily each time they make it to the other side. The result should be a dog who is excitedly running back and forth from person to person, knowing that it will be super rewarding every time. Remember, if the dog doesn't look like they are enjoying themselves, then you are probably doing something wrong!

Once your dog is to the point where they are willing to run back and forth willingly, and you know they are going to come back to you each time, it is time to add in the cue. You will do this by saying their name once in a high-pitched voice, and then giving them their recall command while still employing excited body movements, just to ensure that they do not ignore the cue. As soon as they get to you, they should be rewarded heavily. Please keep in mind that we do not want to repeat our come cue if they do not listen, but rather use our body movements to continue enticing them. If that doesn't work, go to where they are, put them on a leash, and walk them back to where you recalled them from.

LEAVE-IT

WHY TEACH IT?

Just like stay and recall, the leave-it cue is the last vital one to teach in our keeping dogs safe campaign. Not only can this help you get them away from spilled hazardous items like pills, cleaners, and poisonous foods, but it can get them to disengage from prey animals, other dogs, items, and kids if the situation just doesn't seem right. So, whether you are saving their life or just want them to quit trying to get their ball out of the cabinet, leave-it is an instrumental tool for any dog owner's toolbelt.

TRAINER TIP!

When we are teaching the leave-it especially, the timing of our marker and how we deliver our food treat are going to be essential. It is vital that we mark and reward the exact second that our dog chooses to disengage from the treat, even if just momentarily, so that they know what they are being rewarded for. If you miss the opportunity to mark the disengagement early on, it will be very difficult to advance and solidify your leave it. Additionally, the dog should NEVER get what we are asking them to leave alone. After all, we do not want them to think that if they leave something alone, eventually they will be able to have it if they do so, as this will result in them continuing to try to get it and the poisoning of your leave-it cue. Rather, leave-it means leave-it. Therefore, we need to ensure that we are never giving them the treat we are asking them to leave alone as their reward, but rather, rewarding them with the opposite hand for doing so.

HOW TO TEACH IT

To teach leave-it, we are going to start by sitting on the floor with our dog, putting a treat in our hand and then closing it loosely around it. The dog should be able to smell the treat, but not get it out of your hand. Then, you will present your hand to your dog and allow them to start sniffing at it. You can even show it to them before you close your hand if needed. Depending on the dog, they may sniff, lick, paw or even try to nibble at your hand. This is completely normal, and it is vital that you are patient during this time! Usually, when first working on this cue, the dog will take 30 seconds to a minute before they back off even in the slightest (if it takes longer than this, try giving them a no-reward marker). The very second that the dog breaks its attention from the treat in your hand, even if that just means they move their head away slightly or take a second to look at you, mark, and reward with your opposite hand. Again, right at the beginning, we are marking and rewarding even the slightest dis-engagement from our hand.

We will continue doing this 5-10 times, until the dog backs off the treat almost immediately, and then we are going to tie in our cue. When we first introduce the cue, we still want to make sure that we have our hand closed enough that if they try to go for it, we can close our hand and not let them. Then, once they stop trying to go for the baited hand after hearing the cue, we will do the same exercise except now with an open hand. Again, we want to ensure that we can re-close our hand if they try to go after it, as success is our number one goal here.

Once your dog can look at the treat in your open hand and not try to get it, we are going to move to the floor. Remember, dogs are associative learners, so if we want them to leave objects alone that are both in people's hands and on the floor, then we need to make sure we are teaching them in both ways. To do it on the floor, simply put the treat on the floor and cover it with your hand; this way they can see it and smell it, but still not get to it. Then we will repeat the same process until you are able to leave it exposed to them, give them the leave it, and have them not advance at all.

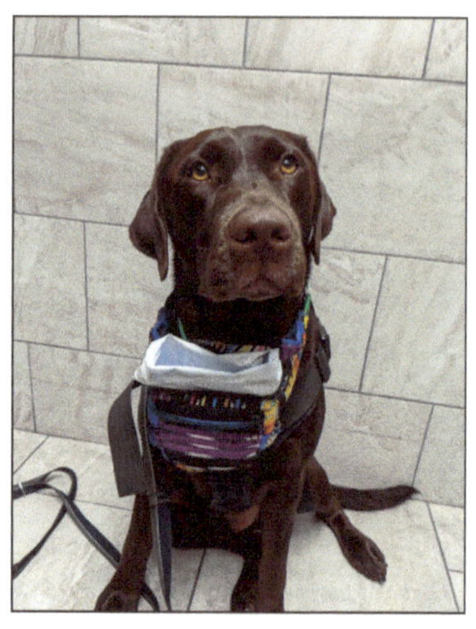

The final step of teaching them to leave-it is to put them on a leash and have some high value items on the floor. Just like moving from your hand to the floor, they need to realize that they still must leave things alone while we are on the move. So, just walk them close to the item, but not close enough that they can grab it, then give them the leave-it cue. If they try to go for the treat, use the same high pitched and excited noises that we did during recall to redirect their attention back to you to get the reward. If they don't get the item, we are still going to reward them, even if it takes a little extra coaxing. Remember, every time we add a new element to our training, you might have to back track slightly to set them up for success and they can build that new association.

THE DIFFERENCE BETWEEN
WAIT AND STAY

As I am sure you already know, staying is one of the most valuable cues that we can teach our dogs. Being able to have them sit or lay in one place while we move freely about is an important skill dogs need to learn so that they are not running off and getting themselves into trouble, or even putting themselves in a dangerous situation. But what if I want to have a command that tells them to wait momentarily before we advance, without necessarily putting them in a fixed position? That is where the difference between wait and stay comes into play.

When I am teaching the stay, I tell the dog that I need them to stay in that exact position until either I return or recall them to me. I am telling them that my movements and actions are independent from theirs, and almost always, I am going to have the dog in either a sit or a down, allowing them to be comfortable while waiting for my return.

In the beginning stages of teaching the stay, I am always going to do it in a manner that allows me to come all the way back to them to reward them, so that they don't break that position and do not get into the habit of following me or anticipating the recall. Once I am sure that the dog understands that they must stay put no matter what, then I will start to add recall to it. Normally, this does not happen until they have already been successful in staying working around various distractions in multiple

settings. This way, I can ensure that they are not going to break that stay because of a distraction and will still be waiting for me to be released regardless of what is going on around them.

Then, when I am teaching the wait, I tell the dog that I need them to pause momentarily, but that they are going to be proceeding with me wherever I go. The main difference here is that I will not really be moving away from the dog at all, and their next movements are still going to be dependent on mine. Some situations where I would use wait instead of stay are entering and exiting cars, buildings, and kennels, while doing food bowl exercises, before we cross the street and need to check for traffic, and when teaching the formal retrieve. As you can see, none of the exercises I use with the wait command require me to move away from the dog, but rather, have them waiting calmly by my side while I ensure that we are okay to proceed. Additionally, with the wait, I do not necessarily care what position their body is in (sit, down, stand) if they have ceased all forward motion with their bodies. However, when first teaching the wait command, I would recommend having them in either the sit or down because they are much less likely to try and push forward than if they were standing.

Although there is not too much difference between these two commands, having two separate ones to use in different situations can make solidifying your stay that much easier. If you only ever use stay to signify that your movements are going to be independent of the dogs, then that is all they will ever know, and they will be much less likely to break that stay around new distractions. However, if your dog gets the belief that stay is sometimes momentarily and sometimes for a long time, how do you expect them to know which one it is you expect when they are around new things that might be scary or exciting for them? That is why having two different cues can be so beneficial, because they will never have to second guess what it is you are asking of them, while simultaneously telling them what they should be expecting next.

DOWN

WHY TEACH IT?

NEXT, WE ARE GOING TO TEACH OUR DOGS HOW TO LAY DOWN. This is another great behavior to have so we can help our dogs settle down and relax, even in stimulating environments. Additionally, teaching the down is a good bonding exercise for dogs and owners, as laying down is one of the most submissive positions a dog can offer you, besides being belly up. Therefore, if you take the time to teach them that lying down is always going to be rewarding for them, they will be more likely to settle into new places easier and rest comfortably knowing that you have their back.

TRAINER TIP!

In my opinion, down is one of the hardest cues to teach dogs, as it requires them to willingly go into a submissive position, and often, not on the most comfortable surfaces. Therefore, it is important that when teaching them down, we are being especially patient and not getting frustrated if they don't get it right away. The more frustrated we get, the more they are going to feel it, and the less likely they will be to want to lay down for you.

HOW TO TEACH IT

To teach our dogs to lie down, once again, we will be using our lure. There are three different ways that we can lure our dogs into the down; from sitting, from standing, and if all else fails, by luring them under our legs.

To lure the dog into the down from the sitting position, start by putting your dog into a sit. Then, you will take your lure and put it against their nose, and then pull the lure slowly from their nose to their front toes, and then slightly out in front of them in an "L" shape. You want to make sure that you are moving slowly and encouraging the dog to slowly crawl their feet out while keeping their butts planted. As the dog follows the treat, they should creep out further and further until eventually, their front elbows touch down on the ground. The moment that their elbows touch the ground, you will mark and reward. Again, if the dog pops right up, that is okay, as we are just working on getting them down into that position.

To lure the dog from the stand, you will start with your dog in a standing position. Then, you will take your lure and put it against their nose, and again you will slowly move it from their nose to their front toes, and then you will push the lure back into them instead of pulling it away. Likely, they will go into a play bow type position with their butts straight up in the air, so you will just keep slowly pushing the lure into them. This will force them to push back further and further with their front paws to get the treat until their butt has no option but to fall to the ground for stability purposes. The moment that happens, you will mark and reward behavior.

If neither one of these luring methods is successful for your pup, we can try to lure them under our legs. You can do this by sitting on the ground and putting your feet up on a wall, chair, couch, or coffee table, creating a 90-degree angle with your legs. Then, you will take your lure and slowly lure them under your legs, as if you were leading them through a tunnel. As they follow the lure under, they will have no choice but to lay down so they can try to crawl, which is when you will mark and reward the behavior.

If the dog is not keeping their nose attached to the lure, I would recommend using a higher value lure that they can't resist (like chopped up hot dogs), or even letting them slowly nibble on it while you lure them. This will keep them engaged on the lure, make them more likely to continue following it, and less likely to get distracted by something else or pull away from it entirely.

If all else fails, you can try to capture the down behavior while you are at home. To do this, you will have to make sure that you always have a couple treats on hand and keep a close eye on your pup. As soon as you see them lying down for any reason, you will mark, reward, and say "good down!". Once you have successfully captured it about 5-10 times (depending on the dog) while tying in the queue at the end, try to see if you are able to lure them again now that they know what is going to get them rewarded.

After you are to the point where the dog is responding to the lure every time, it is time to start fading the lure, add in your verbal cue, and work on your hand signal. To do this, I will give them the down cue, begin luring them, and then stop my lure process as soon as I see them go down. First, you may need to continue luring them all the way, and that is okay! However, gradually you should be able to lure them less and less while still getting the same result. Please note, fading the lure for the down usually takes longer than fading the lure for the sit, so do not get discouraged! For me, the end goal is being able to either just give them the verbal cue or point down towards the ground and have them lay down, as this would be very similar to the first action in the luring process.

If you have one of those dogs that seems to pop up immediately every time, then you likely need to slow down following the completion of the cue. Dogs want to follow us no matter what we are doing, so if we are going all the way to the ground to get them to lay down, they are going to want to follow us as we stand back up. Therefore, once they are in a down position, you might have to start by staying low to the ground with them and giving them another treat every couple of seconds as they stay down. Next, you will stand up slightly, reward them for staying down, stand up a little more, reward them again, and so on, until they are able to stay lying down until you are standing all the way up. While you are working on this, if at any point they get up, you will give your no-reward marker and start the entire process again.

After the lure has been successfully faded and they are able to stay down while we are standing in front of them, we will follow the same procedure with the sit to slowly start building the duration into our down.

HEELING

Perhaps one of the most common issues people bring to me is their dog pulling excessively on the leash. Not only can this make walking them difficult, but also potentially dangerous. Unfortunately, it is also one of the hardest things to teach a dog to do, since there are always a ton of new smells and things to explore. So, let's look at what we need to do to set them up for success, as well as how to go about working on it.

Whenever I am teaching a dog how to heel or walk on a loose leash for the first time, I always try to do it off leash, or in an environment that allows me to drop the dog's leash and have them pull it around. There are four major reasons for this. First, when we are not physically holding a leash, it makes it impossible for us to (even accidentally) issue a leash correction. Instead, it forces us to use nothing but our communication and body language to get the dog to engage with us and stay focused on what we are asking them to do. This is also a great way to work on dog-owner relationships, and get owners used to properly communicating with their dogs.

Second, it forces the dog to start focusing on us and our body movements, as this is what we want them to be responsive to us. For example, if I have a dog that is wandering too far ahead of me, I will lure him back close to me and have him do left-handed circles, which forces them to slow down their pace. If I have a dog that is lagging, I will do circles to the right and encourage them to keep up with me, forcing them to increase their speed. In both situations, I am using my directions and body movements to alter the speed they are moving at.

Third, if we "give the dog permission" to roam about freely on a leash right away, it is much harder to get them to give up that freedom later when we ask them not to pull. Again, think of this as children, where it is always easier to give them more freedom than it is to take it away. Therefore, if we work on them paying attention to us and walking with us even when not on a leash, once we add the leash, they already know what is expected of them.

The final reason is that most owners would like to have the ability to take their dogs with them places off leash, even if it is just going to the mailbox or going for a walk on a nice summer day. If a dog learns how to heel off-leash right off the bat, not only will it allow for more activities the dog and owner can enjoy together but can help with other cues such as recall because the dog is less likely to wander off or get sucked into a distraction and can even eliminate the need some owners feel to use e-collars.

Please watch the attached video to see how I teach heeling using Hershey: https://www.youtube.com/watch?v=KRwEwNqgmWw&list=PLKxv8B-4xyoeaoK5PIKphrvi4qD9ftjP1&index=21

SECTION FOUR:
ADDRESSING "PROBLEM BEHAVIORS"

IMPORTANT THINGS TO REMEMBER ABOUT CHANGING BEHAVIORS

It would be nearly impossible for me to write everything you need to know about dog behavior and how to change it in a single chapter, so instead, I am going to try and give you the most valuable information I have gathered so far during my years of training. The good news is, most of the dogs I ended up working with were dogs with serious behavioral issues, so rest assured that everything I am about to share with you was gained through firsthand experience.

1. Natural behaviors like chewing and certain kinds of barking should never be attempted to be eradicated, but rather kept under control:

If we try to eradicate innate behaviors in our dogs, they can end up with more advanced behavioral issues as we try to keep them from doing what they were born to do, and in the case of chewing, with serious dental issues. For example, if a dog is barking out of fear and they are reprimanded for it, they will learn that barking to say they are scared will not work and they will escalate.

Normally, this means either growling, showing their teeth, or biting, all of which are worse than the original barking behavior. This happens because we have not helped them be less afraid so they don't feel the need to bark, rather, we have taken away their ability to communicate it and now they feel like they must escalate to keep themselves safe.

So, before we start trying to "get rid" of any behavior, we must determine why that behavior is happening, and if the dog's physical and emotional needs are being met.

2. Most behaviors owners consider to be a problem become a problem due to something the owner is or isn't doing:

Therefore, the reason behind the behavior must be determined before we can fix it, as more than likely, there will need to be changes made to the owner's daily routine as well. Please know, this is not a jab at anyone, as I have been guilty of it as well. For example, if we think about excitement jumping, odds are at one point or another the dog was allowed to jump on us when they were puppies, teaching them that if they did, they would get our attention.

So, any time they want your attention now, they assume jumping is going to work because it has in the past. The problem is, now it hurts. So, if we are going to get rid of this behavior entirely, we need to ensure that we are never making it a way for them to get our attention and we are being consistent in our expectations.

3. Most problem behaviors develop due to dogs not getting enough mental and physical stimulation throughout the day, so they go looking for trouble:

Dogs and puppies can be thought of much like young children, and a good rule of thumb is if you don't give them something constructive to do, they will find something self-rewarding to do. Self-rewarding and destructive behaviors usually go hand in hand, so keep them busy.

Generally, owners understand the importance of physical exercise, but if you have a working dog that was bred to work all day every day, the odds of you being able to exercise them enough to fulfill their working needs daily are slim, unless you live on acres of land that the dog has access to all day long. Therefore, mental stimulation is going to be your best friend, as not only do they make your dog smarter, but it drains them physically too. To demonstrate this point, think of how tired young children usually are when they get home from school. Yes, all they did was sit around most of the day, but they were forced to sit still, focus, and apply their brains, which can be even more exhausting than playing. When in doubt, busy dogs are tired dogs, and tired dogs are well-behaved dogs.

4. The less we let our dogs be dogs, the more problem behaviors we are going to see:

Just like with human beings, there are certain things I believe dogs need to feel fulfilled. Whether we always like to admit it or not, dogs are animals, and not humans, which means that they have different needs than we do to feel whole. Having time to run free and explore new environments, follow scents and tracks, mark their territory, chase wild animals, go swimming, play in the mud, meet new people and dogs, and rough house with other dogs are all examples of things I do for my dogs as much as I can to let them be dogs, while simultaneously providing them with mental and physical stimulation. We cannot just expect our dogs to live the exact same life as us and have a well-rounded, happy, and fulfilled life, we need to make sure we are giving them the chance to be themselves.

5. If the dog doesn't respect you as a leader, it is going to be very hard to change bad behavior.

When I say this, I need you to know that there is a big difference between respecting you and fearing you. Fear creates an obedient dog that only listens to avoid consequences, as well as an emotionally repressed dog that is shut down and will usually develop deeper behavioral issues. Emotional suppression, especially fear, is the number one reason behind most of the worst behaviors I see. Respect creates an obedient dog by teaching clear expectations for their behavior through consistency, and an emotionally balanced dog who knows they can express how they are feeling openly without being reprimanded, but rather, understood and guided in the right direction. Being a good leader for your dog is not about intimidation, but about teaching them the difference between right and wrong through mutual respect, guidance, praise, and structure.

6. The number one key to changing a dog's fearful behavior is controlling the way WE respond to our dog's fearful behavior.

I know that I have said this before, but I cannot say it enough, your dog feeds off your energy. So, if they start getting scared, and then you get flustered because of how they normally respond, they will automatically feel the need to escalate because they do not think you are in control of the situation. But, if we can remain in control of ourselves, we can remain in control of the situation and therefore, can work our dogs through those emotional responses in a healthy way and teach them that escalation is not necessary. We do this by reteaching their escalation protocol, with retreating, and checking in with us first on the list.

7. You cannot change fearful behavior without providing positive experiences and associations to whatever they are fearful of.

For example, I see this mistake commonly in people with dog reactive dogs who try to control their dog's behavior through avoidance of other dogs. The problem is, the more we avoid it, the more we are validating the dogs' fear. Rather, we need to set the dog up to have positive experiences with other dogs, even if it is just receiving treats back and forth through a fence, playing the engage/disengage game, or allowing them to watch other dogs play. If the only experiences they ever had with other dogs is what made them fearful, then we need to give them new experiences where they learn they don't have to be.

8. If we use the ways that dogs communicate with one another to communicate with our dogs, it will be easier for them to understand what we are trying to teach them.

One thing Koda taught me is that we need to teach our puppies how to stop, calm down, and choose a different behavior, just like we teach our children. He did this either by use of what we call the "alpha roll" or by backing them into a corner. However, he never did it in a way intended to hurt them, or even scare them, but to let them know "okay, enough is enough, either you can calm down or you can stay pinned, your choice" and he only did it when the dog was in "self-destruct mode". He would not nip, bark at, or bite them, he would just use his body to hold them in place until they chose to calm down, then he would move and let them go on about their way.

To demonstrate how this can be applied to behavior modification in training, I would like to tell you a tale about a pup named Lola. Lola, I believe, was Koda and I's best student, and one of my best teachers. From the time Lola was 9 weeks old, she was food aggressive, she couldn't have her collar grabbed without attacking, she couldn't play without biting, and before bedtime she would go into "tantrums" where she would sprint around crazily and sink her teeth into anything that moved.

Essentially, if Lola didn't like you, or liked what you were asking her to do, she would bite you. Hard. And she was relentless. When I met her, she was 11 weeks old, and her mom already had to have stitches several times. So, I took her home to meet the boys.

One night Lola was in my living room, going through one of her tantrums, and she bit Hershey, then Bruce, then Hershey, like a ping pong ball back and forth. Suddenly, just as Bruce was getting up to "end things", Koda hopped up and got right in her path as she sprinted across the living room. She ran straight into his chest, bounced off, and he literally laid on top of her and held her down, almost like a personal weighted blanket. He used his mouth to hold her head down as she was still trying to attack him, but only with enough pressure to keep her from biting him. Then, he just waited.

After a minute or so of him patiently waiting out her tantrum, she calmed down, so he set her head free but stayed on top of her. Next, she tried to bite him again. Instantly, he gave her an "errrr" and a little check with his nose as if to say "nope, try again." She thought about it for a second, weighed her options, then started licking his face. So, he got up, let her shake it off, then gave her a kiss or two back and sent her on her way with her toy. The simple lesson? You're not going to behave like that anymore. I'm not going to hurt you, but I'm not going to let you get away

with it either. I'm going to kill you with kindness and force you to choose something better. And the best part? It worked. We never had another issue with her biting the boys like that again.

Then the next day I was letting her out to go to the bathroom, and she decided to sneak into the garage. I called her, and she didn't come, so I grabbed my leash and went to get her. When I grabbed onto her collar to put the leash on, she turned and sank her teeth into my thumb. I don't know what came over me, but I thought "what would Koda do?" Well, he wouldn't let her get away with it, and he wouldn't hurt her.

So, there I laid in my garage on top of a puppy who had two canine teeth sunk into one thumb, and two sunk into my finger on the opposite hand as I tried to keep her from biting harder and crushing my fingers. She was throwing a tantrum like you have never seen before, screaming, and trying to scratch me. But I just waited, the same way Koda had.

At a certain point, she started biting harder to try and get me off, and just when I was about to give in, I said "Lola, you need to calm down. This isn't going to work." I don't know if you believe that dogs can understand English, but I do. Or maybe that was my version of the "err", who knows? But the important part is, she calmed right down. I didn't have to yell. I didn't have to hurt her. I just waited out her tantrum. So, I let her up, she tried to lick the blood off my thumb for me, and then I put her on the leash and we both took a much-needed break.

Again, the simple lesson? You're not going to behave like that anymore. You don't have to be afraid of me. I'm not going to hurt you, and you can't just bite me and run away anymore; it isn't going to work. Now, whenever I see her starting to get a little too riled up, I just tell her "Be nice, no teeth", and she will instantly grab a toy to keep playing by herself or lay down for a nap. Lola's biting wasn't an issue again after that.

I guess the point I'm trying to make is that dogs know more than we think they do, and we can learn a lot from them.

From Koda, I learned that you can never fight aggression with aggression, and that if you give the dog an opportunity for a peaceful resolution, they will take it almost every time. But most importantly, sometimes, you just cannot let them win, so they learn "this isn't going to work anymore, and I need to try something else."

9. Sometimes, a behavior cannot be completely changed or modified, and we must focus on maintenance.

I would be a liar if I said that every dog can be helped or changed or be suitable for a normal everyday life.

It's hard to admit that as a trainer and dog lover, but the truth is some dogs cannot be "fixed."

Sometimes dogs experience so much trauma, training, or combination of both, that their brains literally get re-wired. Especially if we are talking about dogs who are much older in age, the odds of being able to give them enough exposure and positive experiences to undo all that trauma are slim, especially if we are not clear on the full background of the dog.

A good example of this are people who rescue bait dogs, and then struggle with them being reactive towards other dogs. Well, if that pup spent their entire life being attacked by other dogs just to "get them pumped up" and then left alone in a kennel the rest of the time while those same dogs barked around them, he is probably scared for his life anytime he sees another dog.

Therefore, rather than trying to make that dog into someone he might never be, a sociable and outgoing guy, we should focus on him being a survivor and giving him HIS best quality of life.

10. If a behavior is self-rewarding to a dog, then the only way it will change is if it becomes unrewarding to them.

I want you to think of this much like alcoholism or drug addiction. Why do they do it? It makes them feel good, or at least better, in that moment. The only way they ever stop doing it is if something good comes into their life and they decide they are ready to change, or something horrible happens and they are forced to change.

Since our dogs lack the consciousness to understand how their behaviors are impacting us or that they could lose us, it is unlikely they are going to change that behavior on their own. And, since we do not want something horrible to happen to them that forces them to change, it is up to us to make that behavior no longer rewarding to them while we are still able to ensure the health and well-being of the dog.

11. When in doubt, working on impulse control and teaching your dog how to self-soothe will help with most problem behaviors.

Impulse control, or patience, is something most dogs, and humans for that matter, lack unless they are taught how to be. Whether this be from watching someone else or having someone else be patient and teach you, patience is a learned behavior. Impulse control exercises force our dogs to be patient and wait calmly for the things they want, which makes it much easier to redirect them in high stimulation environments.

Self-soothing exercises help dogs learn how to come back down from a heightened state of emotion without going into what I like to call "self-destruct" mode. Think of this as very similar to an anxiety attack in humans. They will start hyperventilating, crying, getting physically aggressive, pacing around and starting talking nonsense leaving you wondering what's going on. If you were to yell at them and tell them to sit down, would they suddenly stop having an anxiety attack? Nope. They would now be having an anxiety attack while sitting down. Rather, we need to help them ground themselves, bring them back to the present, and get their breathing under control. The same idea applies to dogs. Often, our dogs will experience fear or excitement so intensely that it brings on a whole slew of other problems because they do not know how to properly funnel all that emotion. If we can teach them how to slow down in that moment long enough for us to direct them to something constructive, then we can manage or correct most behaviors.

12. If you are using positive punishment to change a behavior, you need to make sure that you are doing it with the intention of only having to do it once.

If you have reprimanded your dog for something multiple times and aren't seeing changes, you are either using the tool/punishment incorrectly, you haven't been consistent in your expectations, or the dog is not clear about what they are doing wrong.

As I have said numerous times throughout the book, you cannot punish a dog for something you have never taught them, or for something you have not been consistent about.

Imagine you're an 18-year-old kid that hasn't graduated high school yet. For a while, you have been going and hanging out with your friends on the weekends until 1-2AM in the morning and returning home with no repercussions. Then, suddenly, after months of this going on, you get home one Friday around 2AM and your dad is waiting in the living room to give you the lashing of a lifetime, and you have no idea why.

You didn't do anything different than what you were doing before, except suddenly, he is furious. What would you do? Would you act out more in rebellion? Would you try to blame them for not telling you what time you should be home? Would you be resentful of your dad and not want to be around him for a little while?

Unless your answer is that you would accept full responsibility for not asking what time you should be home even though it's never been an issue before, take that lashing gracefully, and it would in no way have a negative impact on you and your dad's relationship; then you shouldn't expect your dog to respond well to punishment out of convenience.

If you must punish them for the same thing multiple times, there is a miscommunication between you and your dog.

NIPPING

A very common issue that dog owners have is getting their puppy to stop mouthing and biting them. This behavior is known as nipping, and there are many ways that you can approach teaching your puppy that it is not okay. As with some of the other behaviors we have discussed, let's first look at WHY a puppy nips, and then we will discuss how to stop it.

1. Form of communication:

Dogs do not have words, or hands, or any other way of communicating with us besides their body language, vocalizations, and their mouths. Typically speaking, a dog will learn bite inhibition from other members of their "pack", so they are hardly ever trying to hurt you, they have just never been taught that nipping is not an appropriate form of communication with humans and that it can cause you pain.

2. They think they are playing:

If you were to put a couple puppies in the same area and watched them play, I guarantee you a huge amount of that play would result in them biting each other or their toys. Puppies must be taught that the way they play with puppies and the way they play with humans is different, and it is up to you to teach them!

So, how do you teach your puppy not to bite you? As with all my other training guides, I will provide several different options to teach your puppy that this behavior is not okay.

1. Say "OUCH" (startling and breaking the behavior) then give them a tug toy or something else that they can bite and play with you.

The idea is that you are breaking up the action of the puppy and then giving them a viable option of something to chew and bite on while still getting to play with you.

However, keep in mind that this does not work for all puppies, and for puppies who are easily excited or overly rambunctious, this might make them more excited and be tempted to mouth even more.

Therefore, if it doesn't seem to work, move onto the next!

2. Stop playing/ignore them.

If a puppy learns that biting you and playing with you in ways that you do not like will end playtime, then they are less likely to continue doing that behavior.

Therefore, if the puppy starts getting too mouthy with you, it is time to walk away and end playtime for the time being. Remember, your puppy/dog should never be in control of playtime.

3. Put them down for a nap.

Often, when puppies are playing, they will get overly tired, which then makes them mouthier.

If you have a pup that has already been playing for a while without a break, it might be time to put them in their crate for some much-needed rest time.

Just be sure to put them in their kennel with a good chewing toy so that they can take out the rest of that energy in a healthy way, and learn that when they are feeling mouthy, it is time to take a break and lay down with a nice bone.

4. If the other options did not work, then it might be time to resort back to a more natural training style and teach them bite inhibition.

While many people believe that nipping and bite inhibition are the same thing, they are not, and cannot always be approached in the same way.

Nipping is a form of communication and initiating play, while lack of bit inhibition means that they never learned how to control the pressure of their mouth.

Therefore, if you have a dog that is not only nipping, but biting and breaking skin, then there is a good chance that they never learned bite inhibition, and we need to show them that biting hurts us.

As I mentioned earlier, normally, this is something that they would learn from their mother, litter mates, or other adult dogs. However, if you do not have an adult dog that you trust to issue a proper correction, then you will have to teach it to them yourself.

There are several things I have used to address bite inhibition over the years to show them that the action of biting is no longer going to be rewarding to them, all with a lot of success, and I have detailed those for you below:

1. Allow the dog to put your hand in its mouth the way it usually would, then take the skin from either their top or bottom lip and press it firmly against their teeth creating a "bite" affect. It should be hard enough that the dog responds to it, as an under correction is not going to have any effect.
2. Again, allow the dog to put your hand in its mouth, and then pinch the sensitive skin below their tongue using your thumb and pointer finger, with one finger on the bottom of their jaw, and the other inside their mouth under their tongue. Again, it needs to be hard enough that the correction resonates with them, otherwise it will do nothing.
3. If all else fails, bite them back. I know this sounds a little crazy, but it works, because we are establishing that if they continue to bite like that, they are going to be bitten back.

FOR EXAMPLE:

Koda was very independent and headstrong and too smart for his own good.

When I was first working with him on nipping, I tried all the previous techniques, and they would work for a few days, but then once he thought he had the upper hand on me he would do it again.

One day he nipped me hard and left a bruise on my arm, and out of complete frustration I said "NO" and bit him back hard on the tip of his ear. He yelped, looked at me like I was a crazy person, and to this day, he has NEVER put his mouth on me again.

That occurred when he was 6 months old, and he has since passed away at the age of 11.

Sometimes using a dog's own language to your advantage is the fastest way to teach them good behaviors.

BARKING

Do you have a dog that barks at anything and everything that walks by the window? Are you okay with being alerted, but wish they would stop when they are told to do so? Or does your dog bark non-stop when you aren't home which has made your neighbors upset with you?

Here are some tips that you can use to teach your dog that alert barking and being vigilant is okay, but that we need them to be able to settle down when told to do so. As with all my training tips, I will provide different intensity training guides so you can pick what will work best for you and your dog.

1. Break their attention, teach them a "quiet" cue, and reward them for silent behaviors.

When your dog starts barking, go to them and break their attention, whether it be through noises, saying their name, or even leaving their leash attached to them so you can pick it up and guide them away from the window or door. Then, as soon as you have broken their attention from the person/thing, reward them for being quiet and redirecting to you and say "good quiet By doing this you have taught them that it is okay to see things and even bark at them, but that they need to be quiet when we ask them to.

NOTE

Do not sit across the room yelling at your dog while they are ignoring you, all you are doing is teaching them that they do not have to respond to you. If you cannot break their attention by giving them one command, then use the leash method instead so they know that ignoring us is not an option.

2. Play the engage/disengage game with them.

By playing the engage disengage game with them, you can teach them that it is okay to be interested and even excited, but that barking is not necessary. You will do this by slowly exposing them to new distractions, or things that have caused them to bark in the past, allowing them to engage with it visually, and then redirecting them back to you and rewarding them for staying quiet, teaching them alerting is not always necessary.

3. Ensure that they are properly socialized and exposed to all different kinds of items, people, situations, and places.

The more familiar your dog is with a broad range of things, the less likely they are to lose their minds when they see something passing by!

4. Make sure that they are getting enough mental and physical stimulation, as this is usually the number one cause of nuisance behaviors.

A dog that is tired physically and mentally is much less likely to over-react or pass their behavioral threshold and not be able to be redirected. When in doubt, a tired pup is much less likely to become completely overstimulated by a passer-by.

5. Be in control of the environment.

If you know that your dog loves to stare out the front window or door and bark while you are away, consider blocking their access to those areas when you aren't there.

This can be accomplished using a crate, puppy gates, or even a separate room where they are not able to see outside. If we can take away the one thing that is constantly stimulating them, they are less likely to bark consistently.

6. Use a bark collar/e-collar.

Contrary to popular belief, there are bark collars and e-collars that allow you to "correct" your dog, without you ever having to shock them.

Many collars today have super-sonic pitches, beeps, and vibration settings that allow you to modify your dog's behavior without bringing any harm to the dog whatsoever, and providing a hands-off approach whether you are home or away.

These collars work off the principle of negative reinforcement, which means that when the dog starts barking the vibrations of the vocal cords will trigger the collar and begin to emit the tone/beep/vibration creating auditory discomfort to the dog. As soon as they stop barking, the noise will stop.

This teaches the dog that the only way they will be able to shut off the noise is to stop barking. You can also pair this with positive reinforcement, meaning that as soon as you see them stop barking you can reward them by saying "good girl/boy" and then giving a treat.

Since we covered excitement and alert barking, I also wanted to take a little time to address some of the other forms of barking and how I handle them.

Please note that while we cannot shut off barking altogether, there are certain types of barking that should be stopped to keep the dog safe and not potentially put them in an environment where they could get themselves hurt.

1. Demand/Attention barking:

Of all the different kinds of barks we see in our dogs, perhaps the one that gets them into trouble the most often is demand/attention barking. Whether they are doing it to people, or other dogs, this is considered one of the most annoying types of barking, especially to older dogs or those who have low tolerance levels.

Therefore, this is the only type of barking that should try to be eliminated, as it is usually caused by a lack of patience, or a lack of ability to keep themselves stimulated otherwise.

<u>FOR EXAMPLE:</u>

We have all seen a dog that will see another dog with a ball, and then stand in front of them barking incessantly until they have given them the ball.

DO NOT take the ball away from the other dog to give to them, as this would only teach the barking dog that it works and teach the other dog that they must be more protective of whatever they have to make sure the other dog doesn't get it.

If the barking dog cannot be redirected to something else, then they should just be removed from the situation, or corrected for the barking.

This behavior is one of the most common I have seen that gets young dogs especially attacked, so it should not be allowed. Just because they want something, does not mean that they should get it.

2. Aggressive barking:

If you have a dog that becomes offensively aggressive and is barking like that, then they need to be redirected and removed from the situation.

There is no alternate behavior for aggression barking that will be productive. Rather, they need to be redirected and removed until they calm down. Then, you can begin working on SAFE socialization, exposure to new items, and the engage/disengage game to help them learn how to control their emotional reactions and that not everyone they see is something they need to become offensive against.

When in doubt, controlling their environment is going to be the most important in controlling aggressive barking.

3. Fear reactive barking:

This type of barking should be addressed like aggressive barking, and the dog should be redirected and removed until they have calmed down.

Again, alternative behaviors are not really going to be effective with this kind of barking because simply asking them to sit instead is not going to help them calm down or regain control of their fear. We don't just want them to offer a calm behavior, we want them to feel calm and relaxed, and that is going to be achieved by teaching them that even if they are scared, rather than reacting, they can redirect to us for guidance and that we are going to keep them safe and that their extreme level of fear is not necessary.

This is going to be achieved through a lot of proper socialization and exposure work, the engage/disengage game, and showing the dog that their trust in us to keep them safe is greater than their fear of that object.

4. Boredom barking:

If your dog is barking out of boredom it usually means only one thing, they are not getting enough physical and mental stimulation.

Therefore, working on obedience cues with them, ensuring that they have enough stimulation while you are away for the day, taking them on long walks and adventures, and allowing them to play with other well socialized dogs is the best way to approach bored barking.

DIGGING

As we all know, digging is a very natural and self-rewarding behavior for dogs, which can make it a difficult behavior to manage since the reason behind digging is the most important element. Therefore, we are going to take the time to review each of the various reasons behind digging, and the best ways to handle it.

1. Digging out of boredom.

ANTECEDENT ARRANGEMENTS:
Ensure that the dog has had enough physical and mental stimulation by providing them with plenty of engaging toys and games, working on obedience with them, playing fetch, and going for long walks. Block off all areas you do not want the dog to dig into, such as gardens. Refill the holes they have already dug with chicken wire, rocks, or even feces to make those areas unappealing for the dog to dig in again. Do not allow the dog to be outside unsupervised or build a dog run/kennel for them to stay in when you cannot watch them. If the owner is okay with it, recommend building an area specifically for them to dig in.

DIFFERENTIAL REINFORCEMENT OF ALTERNATE BEHAVIORS:

If you catch the dog digging somewhere that they shouldn't be, say no, and redirect them to do something else whether that be playing a game with you, working with you, or taking them to the designated area you have made for them to dig. Be sure that you reward them each time they dig in the appropriate area.

CONSEQUENCES:

If you find out that your dog was digging somewhere they shouldn't once they have already finished, do not scold the dog, as they will not associate the reprimand with digging in the wrong area, just for digging. This will make them want to dig, but in areas that are sneaky. Rather, fill in the holes with something undesirable (rocks, chicken wire, feces), and focus on strict implementation of the antecedents and DRA. If you find your dog still in the process of digging somewhere they shouldn't, say no, and then redirect them to the appropriate digging area or other alternate behavior.

2. Digging to cool off.

ANTECEDENT ARRANGEMENTS:

If the dog is digging to cool off, then many of the antecedents we would normally list do not really apply. Rather, the owner should ensure that the dog has plenty of fresh water and a cool enough area for them to relax in. This can be accomplished by setting up a small kiddy pool with water in it, creating an outdoor kennel run with plenty of shade and a mister or fan (if the dog is spending a long time outside alone in a hot environment), or ensuring that the dog is brought inside to cool off after a play session. The dog should not be left outside unsupervised during hot days so the owner can ensure that they are not overheating and will not be tempted to dig in to be able to cool off.

DIFFERENTIAL REINFORCEMENT OF ALTERNATE BEHAVIORS:

If you catch the dog digging somewhere shady to cool off, you should give them their no-reward marker or a no, and then redirect them to the designated cool area to relax. This way we can teach them that they do not have to dig to cool off, and that we have already provided them with another avenue to take.

CONSEQUENCES:

The dog should never be reprimanded for cooling-off digging, since this would be the owner's error. Instead, they should be told no or given the no reward marker, and then taken to an appropriate area to cool off.

3. Digging to hunt.

ANTECEDENT ARRANGEMENTS:

Dogs that are digging to hunt are always going to be the hardest to work with, since not only is it self-rewarding to them, but their instinct and possibly even what they were bred for. Therefore, we would not want to approach it the same way as some of the others, but rather, focus on them having "jobs" that curb that instinct and allow them to express it in a healthy manner. You should still block off the areas that you absolutely do not want them digging, as well as fill in the holes that they have already dug with something that will deter them from digging in the same spot again. Ensure that the dog has had enough physical and mental stimulation by providing them with plenty of engaging toys and games, working on obedience with them, playing fetch, and going for long walks. Do not allow the dog to be outside unsupervised or build a dog run/kennel for them to stay in when you cannot watch them. Unlike some of the other forms of digging, building them an appropriate area to dig will not really be effective unless that area happens to be right over top of whatever animal's hole it was digging for initially.

DIFFERENTIAL REINFORCEMENT OF ALTERNATE BEHAVIORS:

If you catch the dog digging somewhere that they shouldn't be, say no, and redirect them to doing nose work exercises, playing the 'find it' game, playing fetch, or even just chasing lures. Remember, digging to hunt is very instinctual, so whatever you choose to replace it with must help replace that urge.

CONSEQUENCES:

If you find out that your dog was digging somewhere they shouldn't once they have already finished, do not scold the dog, as they will not associate the reprimand with digging in the wrong area, just for digging. This will make them want to dig, but in areas that are sneaky. Rather, fill in the holes with something undesirable (rocks, chicken wire, feces), and focus on strict implementation of the antecedents and DRA. If you find your dog still in the process of digging somewhere they shouldn't say no, and then redirect them to the appropriate alternate behavior.

4. Digging to bury items.

ANTECEDENT ARRANGEMENTS:

Ensure that the dog has had enough physical and mental stimulation by providing them with plenty of engaging toys and games, working on obedience with them, playing fetch, and going for long walks. Block off all areas you do not want the dog to dig and bury items, such as gardens. Refill the holes they have already dug with chicken wire, rocks, or even feces to make those areas unappealing for the dog to dig in again. Do not allow the dog to be outside unsupervised or build a dog run/kennel for them to stay in when you cannot watch them. If the owner is okay with it, recommend building an area specifically for them to dig in and bury items. You will also want to make sure that you are not leaving the dog unsupervised with items you know they typically like to bury such as bones and other highly scented toys, since these are the ones they are likely to bury and come back to later.

DIFFERENTIAL REINFORCEMENT OF ALTERNATE BEHAVIORS:

If you catch the dog digging somewhere that they shouldn't be, say no, and redirect them to do something else whether that be playing a game with you, working with you, or taking them to the designated area you have made for them to dig. Be sure that you reward them each time they are digging in the appropriate area or playing with their toys without trying to bury them.

CONSEQUENCES:

If you find out that your dog was digging somewhere they shouldn't once they have already finished, do not scold the dog, as they will not associate the reprimand with digging in the wrong area, just for digging. This will make them want to dig, but in areas that are sneaky. Rather, fill in the holes with something undesirable (rocks, chicken wire, feces), and focus on strict implementation of the antecedents and DRA. If you find your dog still in the process of digging somewhere they shouldn't, say no, and then redirect them to the appropriate digging area or other alternate behavior.

IMPULSE CONTROL /
HYPERACTIVITY

When we talk about impulse control, we are talking about helping our dogs learn to control their emotional reactions to stimulus, regardless of the emotion or stimulus being presented. While many believe this is just in relation to things like leash reactivity, the truth is, your dog needs to learn how to control many different emotions if they are going to be happy home dwellers.

Therefore, in this chapter, we are going to cover a couple of the emotions you will likely see most often, and some different impulse control exercises you can do with them to help them stay under control.

The first emotion we are going to see is excitement. Whether they get excited about new people, places, dogs, or items, there are many exercises we can do to help them understand that their excitement is warranted, but that they still need to remain under control even when they are excited and that they will still get rewarded for doing so. Generally, these dogs are very hyper, very sociable, and think everything and everyone wants to be part of their life.

The second emotion most likely to plague our dogs is fear. While addressing fear issues is going to take a combination approach of exposure, engage/disengage games, counter conditioning, and desensitization, helping them control their fear before it escalates will help them not get

into the manic stage, and even possibly avoid them getting fully reactive. These dogs tend to fall into the timid category, are not usually very outgoing or explorative, and often come from homes or situations where abuse occurred.

Third, and potentially the hardest to work on, are going to be the dogs who have extremely high prey drives or aggressive tendencies. hese are the types of dogs that will play fetch for hours on end, dig up the yard chasing animals under the surface, or those who show an offensive threat posture when they are confronted with new things.

Most commonly, these types of dogs are going to belong to one of the working groups, and they are looking for a job to do, so they pursue the things that come to them instinctually.

One of the most important things to remember when working on impulse control is that it is vital you understand the emotional response you are working through before you start.

Obviously, you would not want to mistake a dog who is fear reactive for a dog who is displaying aggressive tendencies, because the way you handle it could end up making them even more reactive, or even escalating their behavior to the point of lunging or biting.

Therefore, if you are ever unsure of where a behavior is originating from, it is always best to seek guidance from a behaviorist or more advanced trainer.

Now that we have all that out of the way, let's look at a variety of impulse control exercises you can implement, and the emotions they work best on:

Exercise	Excitement	Fear	Prey Drive / Agg Tend.
Ignoring them, waiting for a calm behavior, rewarding	X		
Formal Retrieving	X		X
Engage/Disengage Game	X	X	X
Waiting for Food Bowl	X	X	X
Calming exiting car, house, or kennel	X	X	X
Take it, Tug, Out sequence	X		X
People Greeting Exercise	X	X	X (only if the dog is not people aggressive)
Neutral Dog Exercises	X	X	X (if dog aggressive, make sure enough distance is left that the dog cannot lunge)
Working Alongside other dogs	X	X	
Settling Exercises	X	X	X
Rally	X	X (builds confidence in handler)	
Agility	X	X (builds confidence in dog)	X (only if it can be done in a safe environment)
Nose Work Exercises	X		X
Exposure Work (at the dog's pace)	X	X (extremely important to move slowly and make very positive)	X
Socialization (at the dog's pace)	X	X	X (only if it can be done safely, never put anyone else in harm trying to socialize your dog)
Leave-It Exercises	X		X (be sure to do a lot of things with moving objects, have to learn they are not allowed to pursue anything that moves)

FEAR REACTIVITY – CASE STUDY ON LUNA

Fear reactivity is one of the most difficult, and sometimes frustrating things to work on with dogs, yet it is way more common than you think. Because of this, I decided to make a video documentary about an 11-month-old black lab named Luna that I worked with recently. Here I will talk you through how and why I do everything and give you some tools to start better understanding and working with fear reactive dogs.

Let's Talk Fear Reactivity:

https://www.youtube.com/watch?v=7R-rixg9_VRg&list=PLKxv8B-4xyoeaoK5PIKphrvi4qD9ftjP1&index=17

Lessons 1, 2, and 3:

https://www.youtube.com/watch?v=f9WUWqt1y-fA&list=PLKxv8B-4xyoeaoK5PIKphrvi4qD9ftjP1&index=16

Lessons 4 and 5:

https://www.youtube.com/watch?v=KcjkztQgogQ&list=PLKxv8B-4xyoeaoK5PIKphrvi4qD9ftjP1&index=18

Off-Leash Work Around Other Dogs:

https://www.youtube.com/watch?v=2eqqvF3zJLE&list=PLKxv8B-4xyoeaoK5PIKphrvi4qD9ftjP1&index=19

Moderating Luna's Play:

https://www.youtube.com/watch?v=IvtNSb-KQv6g&list=PLKxv8B-4xyoeaoK5PIKphrvi4qD9ftjP1&index=20

WORKING WITH LITTERMATES – CASE STUDY ON BELLA AND CASH

VIDEOS:

Case study - https://youtu.be/pL6C6bLxxjs?si=kHRr30sjklDwVrFF
Lesson 1 - https://youtu.be/elQrwF0M33o?si=qsAvH4WnmER3nJU9
Lesson 2 - https://youtu.be/y_1_DBbAG04?si=1V8E_HzoJiImo3Wg
Lesson 3 - https://youtu.be/cV3ct5LP774?si=G0Of7mvtJUg0PQzK
Lesson 4 - https://youtu.be/atO1jfqe5CQ?si=Qw3e8fUWjdGqJ79k
Lesson 5 - https://youtu.be/3HM_JA7mvn8?si=dqIgun9EtNuztVs7

SEND HOME NOTES TO THE OWNER:

During their time here with me, we worked on a ton of stuff. Not all their basic obedience progressed as far as I might have hoped, however, we put a much stronger emphasis on things like leave-it, impulse control, not seeking attention to bad behaviors, and being able to just "settle" when there isn't anything else going on. As far as obedience is concerned though, we worked on sit, down, stay, leave-it, Loose leash walking, outdoor recall off leash, their no-reward marker, and not freaking out any time you grab or put pressure on their collar.

Now, here is everything I learned about them during their stay.

Bella: For the most part, all of Bella's unwanted behaviors seem to come from her prey drive and a lack of stimulation/needing something to do. When Bella is properly stimulated, her behavior is pretty excellent, although she can be very persistent in certain situations such as seeking out and eating poop, finding things to chew on she shouldn't be (although when she had knuckle bones present, she redirected herself to those almost all the time), and trying to go after everything that moves (mop/broom/vacuum/spray bottle).

In the case of poop eating, I would recommend a couple of things (this applies to both dogs).

1. Possibly check with your veterinarian to ensure that their nutritional needs are being met.
2. Ensure there are always other things for her to chew on, especially ones that are highly scented like knuckle bones.
3. Since eating poop is often seen as an attention seeking behavior, ensuring that they are getting enough exercise and mental stimulation will be important.

When it comes to Bella's jumping, again, this is an attention seeking behavior, because she has found that it worked in the past to get her attention. Therefore, it is important that there is a zero-tolerance policy about jumping, even during play time. Since it is a self-rewarding behavior for her, she needs to be retaught that jumping is not going to get her rewarded, but that nice calm behavior will. So, if she starts to jump, she needs to be told "NO" and ignored until she offers another behavior, such as sitting or just keeping all four feet on the ground before she is rewarded. If she is jumping sporadically, then a correction will likely be needed, such as raising your knee and letting her jump into it.

With Bella's nipping, there has to be a zero-tolerance policy. She will need to be reprimanded every single time her teeth touch someone's skin, as it is self-rewarding behavior that she needs to know is not what is going to get her what she wants. She tried a couple of times when she was here and got better and better. We also used the "be nice" and "no teeth" commands to remind her when she was in exciting situations.

We put a huge focus on her not attacking household items, as well as the kitten. She responded extremely well to the leave it and the no reward markers, and I was able to work her through the broom, the mop, spray bottles, basketball, a kid on a bike, the kitten, and several other items while she was here. While she is not perfect at this by any means, she at least listens now, and you can get her to stop if she does try to go after it.

Cash: Pretty much all of Cash's unwanted behaviors are a result of him being under stimulated and seeking attention. You can tell that he is a working dog, and he not only wants a job, but needs one. For Cash to be a well-behaved dog, he is going to need a lot more stimulation than Bella does, whether this comes in the form of working or playing the fetch game. Additionally, if you do not give him something to do, he is going to go find it, and this is likely why you see him engaging in chewing, attacking Bella randomly, and counter surfing behaviors. If he has something to do, like a high value chew toy, he is pretty good at keeping himself entertained.

One thing Cash really struggles with is being told "NO". He likes to have his way, and he will persistently try to get it unless you guide him to give up and just relax. I saw this most commonly in the evenings when I would finally take his ball away and make him start calming down for bed, at which time he would almost always either go find something to try and chew on, jump on the table/counter, or try to attack Bella. I also saw the same behavior outside when we were playing fetch and one of the other dogs would get the ball. Therefore, it is important that we keep an eye on him during these times, as we do not want him to keep seeking bad behaviors as coping mechanisms.

I worked a lot with Cash on his ball fixation and used it to my advantage to give him a "job" in the form of nice fetching. The more you work with Cash during play time and force him to use his self-control, the faster he will get tired out, and he will get more tired than usual. We also worked a lot on his fixation to attack Bella, especially when he doesn't get his way, and while he still tries sometimes, I have gotten him to the point where just saying his name or "be nice", is enough for him to disengage from her.

Both Cash and Bella are too smart for their own good, meaning that they are going to try and test you every step of the way. It is vitally important that we do not "let them win" in these moments. Each time you ask them to do something, they need to listen, regardless of what it is you are asking them to do. Each time they ignore you and keep doing it, they will just learn that they don't have to listen to you when you tell them to do something.

Additionally, since they are littermates, they are constantly learning and adapting from one another, as well as leaning on one another when they want to do something they aren't supposed to. In simple terms, they think that they are allowed to do whatever they want, because their sibling has their back, which makes it even more important that they are not allowed to "win."

WHY WILL MY DOG LISTEN TO MY SIGNIFICANT OTHER AND NOT ME?

WHEN BRINGING A NEW DOG HOME, IT IS IMPORTANT TO remember that dogs operate in a pack mentality, meaning that there are going to be "Alpha" and "Beta" members of the family. While there are many people that believe this is not true, it becomes painfully obvious if you spend enough time watching them and how they operate in large groups. Therefore, typically speaking, one partner will tend to be more of a disciplinarian while the other will be more affectionate, such as the good cop and bad cop routine. Because of this, the dog figures out quickly what they can and cannot get away with when with each partner, and they will take as much advantage of it as they can.

This is why it is important that both partners decide on what the standards for the dog will be, and work on them together and be consistent. For example, if dad never lets the dog on the couch at all, but mom will let it up there to snuggle when dad is not home, who do you think the dog is more likely to listen to when you catch him on the couch when he isn't supposed to be? Dad, because he set that precedent from the very beginning.

A lot of people will say that they just don't have the heart to be mean to or punish their dog, but the truth is, you don't have to be mean or punish them. You must be consistent. Just like children, if you let them get away with whatever they want, why would they suddenly start listening when you decide you've had enough? Being consistent with your puppy does not mean you cannot have a happy and loving relationship with them. It just means you are creating a standard for their behavior right from the beginning, which will make the chances of them misbehaving less likely as you continuously reward them for the behaviors you want.

The good news is, if you are already having some of these issues with your dog, there are some things that you can do to help them learn that they must listen to you! Remember, these things should be done by the owner who feels as though they are not being listened to. Not only will it help them build a better relationship with their pup but give them the tools to be able to manage all their behaviors.

1. Start by playing the name game with them, and only rewarding them when they respond the first time, every time.

Sometimes, owners assume that the dog knows their name and that they should be responding to them when they say it. However, unless you have taken the time to teach the dog its name and ensured that they know they must respond each time, then how can you be sure that they think their name is "Koda" and not "Koda Koda Koda Koda."

2. Teach them a no-reward marker.

This will give you a way to tell the dog that you do not like what they are doing, and that you would like them to try and offer you something else. It is always important to be able to communicate what we don't like while simultaneously rewarding them for the behaviors we do!

3. Hand feed them their food.

This is a huge bonding exercise between dog and owner, and teaches them that if they want their food, then they must come to you to do it. Trust and respect are a huge deal in terms of whether a dog is going to listen to you, and if you are in ultimate control of their meals, then they will soon learn that if they do not trust and respect you, that they are not going to be fed.

4. Work basic obedience skills with them.

The more you work with a dog, the more they are going to trust and respect you as their "leader". Dogs, whether they realize it or not, want your guidance in most, if not all situations. Therefore, the more you work them and help them realize that you can give that guidance, and they will be rewarded for it, the more likely they are to listen to you.

5. Try not to let your dog be in positions where they are over top of you, or can look down on you, especially if there are behavioral issues involved.

If you have spent enough time around dogs, you will notice that whenever they feel defiant, or even dominant, they will try to position themselves in a spot that is higher than the other person/dog, whether that means getting up on a couch, bed, or even going up a few stairs and then looking down. What this is doing is establishing "hey, I'm over top of you, what are you going to do about it now?". Depending on the behavioral issue at hand, this can be

seen as a sort of status challenge, and if possible, should be avoided.

6. Don't step around your dog if they are in the way, simply ask them to move.

I know a lot of people get into the habit of not wanting to move their dog because "they look so cute!", but the truth is, if you are already having respect issues with them, it is only going to make it worse. Each time you move around them you are giving them a little more power and letting them know that they do not have to respect you or get out of your way when necessary.

I know that there are a lot of people out there that think pack mentality doesn't exist, and I hate to break it to those people, but they are wrong. In any real pack, the leader is never going to step over or go around another member, but rather, force them to move.

7. Be in control of when playtime starts and ends.

I know that it seems selfish to be the one that ends playtime, especially with puppies, but again, we need them to learn that they are on our schedule, and not the other way around. The more you let them control even simple things, such as play, the more they will think they should be in control in other situations as well.

8. Do not engage in activities with them that are too rough, or give them the opportunity to be mouthy, chase you, or be on top of you.

We all like to wrestle and play with our dogs, and I am by no means saying that you should not do these things ever with your dog. But, if it gets to the point that they are nipping at you, trying to tackle you, or anything else like that, play time needs to end.

Nipping and tackling are both things that dogs will do to other dogs when they are trying to control/direct their behavior, so allowing them to do that to you tells them that they should be able to dictate play time, and we do not want that.

ACKNOWLEDGEMENTS

I first started this book as a training manual to help assist my clients in being able to understand their dogs and work through their issues. Many of them were so wonderful in assisting me by allowing me to work with their dogs and record them for lessons, or in helping provoke ideas for many of the chapters in this book. So, to all my clients who helped me, thank you for helping me become the trainer I am today.

Throughout the years, my training business has changed many times. Despite all these changes, I always had an amazing level of support and encouragement from my closest friends and family. Without them, I might have never had the courage to go through with this new endeavor, and certainly not written my own book. So, to my closest friends and family, thank you for always believing in me and what I am capable of, even when I doubt myself.

Next, I would like to thank my friend and business partner, Billie Lawrence. Billie went from being one of my students, to my friend, and now my business partner, and I could not thank her enough for all that she has done to help make this dream a reality. So, Billie, thank you for seeing my vision, sharing my passion, and helping me bring it to life.

Finally, I would like to thank my boys. Koda, Bruce, and Hershey have not only been instrumental in helping me become a better person and trainer, but also in helping so many other dogs learn how to be good dogs. Over the years, I have brought puppy after puppy home, and they have welcomed them into our home and treated them as our own. All the while, being the best friends a girl could ask for. So, to my boys, thank you for loving me, for teaching me, and for never leaving my side.

ABOUT THE AUTHOR

Growing up, I always had a love for animals far beyond that of a normal kid. I always had at least a couple of animals. I would carry around dictionaries of different dog breeds and horses, bring home every animal I found, and was determined to be a veterinarian when I grew up. Unfortunately, some unforeseen events happened when I was 17 that changed the trajectory of my life forever, and I wound up enlisting in the Marine Corps.

I started training dogs professionally about 8 years ago, right after I got out of the Marine Corps in 2016. I got certified as a Professional Dog Trainer through Animal Behavior College, then soon after took a position as the head obedience trainer at a large dog boarding facility in Texas, which had a strong focus on gun dogs. Here, not only did I work with hunting dogs, but also taught group and private lessons, focusing on everything from basic obedience to solving problem behaviors. While I really loved this work, I was not a huge fan of some of the "old style" training procedures and sought to find ways to teach the dogs the same skills, without the old harsh methods. However, I am thankful for my training experience there, as I learned not only how to properly use every tool you can imagine, but also got a much better understanding of when and why they should be used. While we would all like to believe that everything can be solved with positive reinforcement alone, my time out in the training arena as showed me otherwise, and I am thankful that I have the skills and knowledge to help all the dogs that come by way, regardless of what is going on with them.

Additionally, I had always wanted to work with service dogs, specifically those trained to help mitigate the symptoms of Post Traumatic Stress Disorder in Veterans. This led me to leave my job at the boarding facility, where I became the Veteran Liaison and Puppy Program Manager for a non-profit, also in Texas. While I loved this line of work and getting to take the puppies all the way from start to finish, I soon learned that not everyone was in this line of work for the same reasons I was, and eventually I ended up as an independent trainer.

As a trainer now, my only focus is this: Facilitating the healthiest relationship possible between dogs and their owners so they can live a long, happy, and prosperous life with one another. While I do not take on too many clients nowadays, I feel a lot of pride in switching my focus to helping mold the next generation of trainers. Although I have had the opportunity to help many dogs and owners alike along my journey, I realize that I am only a small crumb in the cookie jar of dog trainers, 

and feel as though I will be able to help even more dogs by ensuring that the next generation of trainers are confident, knowledgeable, and have the proper tools and skill sets to help all the dogs that come their way.